CAMBRIDGE
UNIVERSITY PRESS

Physics

for Cambridge IGCSE™

ENGLISH LANGUAGE SKILLS WORKBOOK

David Sang, Timothy Chadwick, Deepak Choudhary,
Darrell Hamilton & Fiona Mauchline

CAMBRIDGE
UNIVERSITY PRESS

University Printing House, Cambridge CB2 8BS, United Kingdom

One Liberty Plaza, 20th Floor, New York, NY 10006, USA

477 Williamstown Road, Port Melbourne, VIC 3207, Australia

314–321, 3rd Floor, Plot 3, Splendor Forum, Jasola District Centre, New Delhi – 110025, India

103 Penang Road, #05–06/07, Visioncrest Commercial, Singapore 238467

Cambridge University Press is part of the University of Cambridge.

It furthers the University's mission by disseminating knowledge in the pursuit of education, learning and research at the highest international levels of excellence.

www.cambridge.org
Information on this title: www.cambridge.org/9781108826792

First edition 2022

20 19 18 17 16 15 14 13 12 11 10 9 8 7 6 5 4 3 2 1

Printed in Italy by Rotolito S.p.A.

A catalogue record for this publication is available from the British Library

ISBN 978-1-108-82679-2 English Language Skills Workbook Paperback with Digital Access (2 Years)

Additional resources for this publication at www.cambridge.org/go

Illustrations by Tech-Set Ltd

DEDICATED TEACHER AWARDS

Teachers play an important part in shaping futures. Our Dedicated Teacher Awards recognise the hard work that teachers put in every day.

Thank you to everyone who nominated this year; we have been inspired and moved by all of your stories. Well done to all of our nominees for your dedication to learning and for inspiring the next generation of thinkers, leaders and innovators.

Congratulations to our incredible winners!

WINNER

Regional Winner Middle East & North Africa	Regional Winner Europe	Regional Winner North & South America	Regional Winner Central & Southern Africa	Regional Winner Australia, New Zealand & South-East Asia	Regional Winner East & South Asia
Annamma Lucy GEMS Our Own English High School, Sharjah - Boys' Branch, UAE	**Anna Murray** British Council, France	**Melissa Crosby** Frankfort High School, USA	**Nonhlanhla Masina** African School for Excellence, South Africa	**Peggy Pesik** Sekolah Buin Batu, Indonesia	**Raminder Kaur Mac** Choithram School, India

For more information about our dedicated teachers and their stories, go to
dedicatedteacher.cambridge.org

CAMBRIDGE
UNIVERSITY PRESS

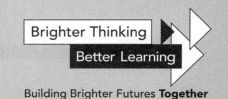

Brighter Thinking
Better Learning

Building Brighter Futures **Together**

> Contents

> How to use this series

We offer a comprehensive, flexible array of resources for the Cambridge IGCSE™ Physics syllabus. We provide targeted support and practice for the specific challenges we've heard that learners face: learning science with English as a second language; finding the mathematical content within science difficult; and developing practical skills.

The coursebook provides coverage of the full Cambridge IGCSE Physics syllabus. Each chapter explains facts and concepts, and uses relevant real-world examples of scientific principles to bring the subject to life. Together with a focus on practical work and plenty of active learning opportunities, the coursebook prepares learners for all aspects of their scientific study. At the end of each chapter, examination-style questions offer practice opportunities for learners to apply their learning.

The Cambridge IGCSE Physics digital teacher's resource contains detailed guidance for all topics of the syllabus, including common misconceptions and identifying areas where learners might need extra support, as well as an engaging bank of lesson ideas for each syllabus topic. Differentiation is emphasised with advice for identification of different learner needs and suggestions of appropriate interventions to support and stretch learners. The teacher's resource also contains support for preparing and carrying out all the investigations in the Cambridge IGCSE Physics Practical Workbook, including a set of sample results for when practicals aren't possible.

The teacher's resource also contains scaffolded worksheets and unit tests for each chapter. Answers for all components are accessible to teachers for free on the Cambridge GO platform.

The skills-focused workbook has been carefully constructed to help learners develop the skills that they need as they progress through their Cambridge IGCSE Physics course, providing further practice of all the topics in the coursebook. A three-tier, scaffolded approach to skills development enables learners to gradually progress through 'focus', 'practice' and 'challenge' exercises, ensuring that every learner is supported. The workbook enables independent learning and is ideal for use in class or as homework.

The Cambridge IGCSE Physics Practical Workbook provides learners with additional opportunities for hands-on practical work, giving them full guidance and support that will help them to develop their investigative skills. These skills include planning investigations, selecting and handling apparatus, creating hypotheses, recording and displaying results, and analysing and evaluating data.

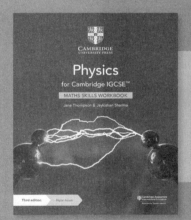

Mathematics is an integral part of scientific study, and one that learners often find a barrier to progression in science. The Maths Skills for Cambridge IGCSE Physics write-in workbook has been written in collaboration with the Association for Science Education, with each chapter focusing on several maths skills that learners need to succeed in their physics course.

Our research shows that English language skills are the single biggest barrier to learners accessing international science. This write-in workbook contains exercises set within the context of Cambridge IGCSE Physics topics to consolidate understanding and embed practice in aspects of language central to the subject. Activities range from practising using comparative adjectives in the context of measuring density, to writing a set of instructions using the imperative for an experiment investigating frequency and pitch.

⟩ How to use this book

Throughout this book, you will notice lots of different features that will help your learning. These are explained below. Answers are accessible to teachers for free on the 'supporting resources' area of the Cambridge GO website.

INTRODUCTION

This sets the scene for each chapter.

LEARNING INTENTIONS

These set out the learning intentions for each exercise. Each exercise will help you to develop both your English skills and your physics skills.

KEY WORDS

Key vocabulary and definitions are given at the start of each investigation. You will also find definitions of these words in the Glossary at the back of this book.

Exercises

These help you to develop and practise your English skills alongside your physics skills.

LANGUAGE FOCUS

These give you more information about parts of the English language that you may find challenging, to help you use English more fluently.

LANGUAGE TIP

The information in these boxes will help you complete the questions using correct English, and give you support in areas that you might find difficult.

⟩ Supplement content

Where content is intended for students who are studying the Supplement content of the syllabus as well as the Core, this is indicated using the arrow and the bar, as on the left here.

> Introduction

Welcome to this workbook, which will help you with your study of physics using English. To make good progress in your studies in physics, it will help if you can also use the English language well in a way that is appropriate to science. If you can read English well, you can understand what is written in your physics coursebook easily. If you can write and speak English well, you can share your knowledge about physics with others easily.

This workbook will help you understand some important topics in physics. It will also help you develop your skills in English. The exercises will give you practice in both things at the same time.

The exercises will help your English skills in different ways. They will:

- help you understand the meaning of important words

- help you to use certain types of words correctly, like nouns and adjectives

- help you to construct sentences correctly

- help you to construct whole passages of text

- give you practice in reading text and extracting information from it.

The areas of English covered in this book have been chosen because they are useful to understand and discuss the subject of physics. Aspects of language are discussed directly to help you understand certain exercises, and to explain why these aspects are useful to you as you learn physics. There is also a Skills and Support section at the start of this book that provides an overview of the English language skills covered. You can refer to this section at any point to help you find out more about the language skills discussed within the chapters. You will be able to link these explanations to the content of your English language course.

We hope you enjoy using this book, and that it helps you progress in your studies of physics and English.

Note for teachers:

Additional teaching ideas for this English Language Skills Workbook are available on Cambridge GO, downloadable with this workbook and the Cambridge IGCSE Physics Teacher's Resource. This includes engaging activities to use in lessons, with guidance on differentiation and assessment.

Answers to all questions in this English Language Skills Workbook are also accessible to teachers at www.cambridge.org/go

> Skills and support

Introduction

This section includes information about English language skills, which are essential for you in order to understand science concepts and to communicate your science ideas effectively to others.

You can use this English reference section at any time to support your studies in science.

Quick reference guide

Grammar	Use	Example
Noun (n)	A word to show the name of a person, place or object.	A *physicist*. A *science laboratory*. An *electron*.
Verb (v)	A word to show an action or state.	I *measure* the time period of an oscillation. We *calculate* the speed.
Adjective (adj)	A word to describe the quality or state of a noun.	The *negative* charge. The *reflective* surface.

Present simple

The present simple is used to talk about facts and things that are generally true. It can also be used to talk about habits and routines and often with verbs of senses and perception, for example: *think, hurt, understand.*

There are different groups of verbs in English, for example, the verb *to be,* regular verbs and irregular verbs.

The verb *to be* can be used to describe somebody or something and can be followed by adjectives and nouns.

	Affirmative	Negative	Question
I	am	am not	Am I…?
He, she, it	is	is not	Is he, she, it…?
You, we, they	are	are not	Are you, we, they…?

Example sentences:

Affirmative	Negative	Question
I am a scientist.	I am not a scientist.	Am I a scientist?
It is an electron.	It is not an electron.	Is it an electron?
They are insulators.	They are not insulators.	Are they insulators?

Regular verbs in the present

Sentences with *I*, *you*, *we* and *they*, just use the basic verb form, for example, *measure, record, start.*

Sentences with *he*, *she* and *it*, you must add *-s* or *-es* to the end of the verb.

With verbs ending in a consonant (b, c, d, f, g…) + *y*, change the *y* to an *i* and then add *-es* in the affirmative form when it follows, *he, she, it.* For example, *it flies.*

With verbs ending in a vowel (a, e, i, o, u) + *y* add an *s* when it follows, *he, she, it.* For example, *he observes, she researches.*

When the verb ends in *-ch*, *-ss*, *-sh*, *-x* or *-zz* also add *-es* in the affirmative form when it follows *he, she, it.* For example, *she watches.*

	Affirmative	Negative	Question
I, you, we, they	I *calculate* the velocity. We *study* Ohm's law. They *observe* the solar system.	I don't *calculate* the velocity. We don't *study* Ohm's law. They don't *observe* the solar system.	Do I *calculate* the velocity? Do we *study* Ohm's law? Do they *observe* the solar system?
He, she, it	He *calculates* the velocity. She *studies* Ohm's law. It *observes* the solar system.	He doesn't *calculate* the velocity. She doesn't *study* Ohm's law. It doesn't *observe* the solar system.	Does he *calculate* the velocity? Does she *study* Ohm's law? Does it *observe* the solar system?

Irregular verbs in the present

Some verbs are irregular, meaning they don't follow the usual rules. Some examples of irregular verbs are, *have*, *go* and *do*.

	Affirmative	Negative	Question
I, you, we, they	I *have* an ammeter. We *go* into orbit. They *do* investigations.	I don't *have* an ammeter. We don't *go* into orbit. They don't *do* investigations.	Do I *have* an ammeter? Do we *go* into orbit? Do they *do* investigations?
He, she, it	She *has* an ammeter. He *goes* into orbit. It *does* investigations.	She doesn't *have* an ammeter. He doesn't *go* into orbit. It doesn't *do* investigations.	Does she *have* an ammeter? Does he *go* into orbit? Does it *do* investigations?

Be careful with irregular plurals that are from Greek and Latin origins; make sure you know which form is singular and which is plural. Be sure to use *is* with the singular and *are* with the plural form.

A *vertex* is a point where particles collide and interact. *Vertices* involve the interaction between a photon and an electron.

Spelling rules for plurals

Most plural nouns in English are formed by adding *-s* or *-es* to the singular noun:

force – forces   movement – movements

When a singular noun ends with a consonant and a *-y*, the *-y* becomes *-ie* before you add the *-s*:

density – densities   velocity – velocities

Some scientific words are from Latin or Greek and have different endings.

Nouns ending in -*us* in the singular form usually end with -*i* in the plural form:

nucleus – nuclei   radius – radii

Nouns ending -*a* in the singular form may end with -*ae* in the plural form:

antenna – antennae   nebula – nebulae

Nouns ending in -*is* in the singular form usually end with -*es* in the plural form:

Thesis – theses   crisis – crises

Nouns ending in -*on* or -*um* in the singular form may end with -*a* in the plural form:

criterion – criteria   phenomenon – phenomena

Present simple passive

Present simple passive is used to talk about some actions that occur in the present or repeated habits or simple statements of fact. The present simple passive puts the emphasis on what happens, rather than who did the action. It is possible to say who did the action by using *by* + *who* / *what*.

The present simple passive is formed by using the verb *to be* (*am* / *is* / *are*) + past participle.

Steam *is created* when water boils.

Gas pressure *is caused* by gas particles reaching the walls of the container they are in.

A circular magnetic field *is created* around a wire when a current flows in it.

Present continuous

The present continuous is used to talk about what is happening now.

The present continuous is formed by stating the subject + verb *to be* (*am*, *is*, *are*) and the main verb + ing.

Affirmative

Subject	Verb to be	Verb + ing
I	am	observing.
He, she, it	is	calculating.
You, we, they	are	measuring.

Negative

Subject	Verb to be	Verb + ing
I	am not	observing.
He, she, it	is not	calculating.
You, we, they	are not	measuring.

Question

Verb to be	Subject	Verb + ing
Am	I	observing?
Is	he, she, it	calculating?
Are	you, we, they	measuring?

Example sentences:

	Affirmative	Negative	Question
I, you, we, they	I *am measuring* the length of the track.	I *am* not *measuring* the length of the track.	*Am* I *measuring* the length of the track?
	We *are measuring* the length of the track.	We *are* not *measuring* the length of the track.	*Are* we *measuring* the length of the track?
He, she, it	She *is measuring* the length of the track.	She *is* not *measuring* the length of the track.	*Is* she *measuring* the length of the track?
	It *is measuring* the length of the track.	It *is* not *measuring* the length of the track.	*Is* it *measuring* the length of the track?

Spelling

With most verbs in the present continuous, just add *-ing*. But sometimes we double the last letter or remove the last letter before adding *-ing*.

Basic rule		Just add *-ing* to the base verb:
experiment	→	experimenting
find	→	finding
show	→	showing

If the verb ends in consonant + stressed vowel + consonant, double the last letter:

s	t	o	p
	consonant	stressed vowel	consonant

plan	→	planning
refer	→	referring
get	→	getting

This rule does not apply when the last syllable of the verb is not stressed:

open	→	opening

If the verb ends in vowel + consonant + *e*, remove the *e* before adding *-ing*.

describe	→	describing
analyse	→	analysing

Verb + ing

You can use the present continuous to say who or what is doing something now. You can also use verb + *ing* without the agent (who or what is doing the action).

I *see* the ice melting.

They *saw* the temperature decreasing.

We *experienced* floating in a zero-gravity capsule.

Also, verb + *ing* is used after certain verbs, for example:

Start, stop, finish, suggest, recommend, avoid, keep, risk, enjoy, delay, involve, remember

Start timing the experiment.

The lamp *stopped emitting* light.

I have *finished operating* the motor.

They *suggest increasing* the voltage.

I *recommend observing* the pressure increase.

We should *avoid opening* the capsule too soon.

We must *keep checking* the results at different stages of the experiment.

Don't *risk creating* a vacuum.

We *enjoyed learning* about electromagnetism.

We *delayed completing* the circuit until we had all of the components.

Electrical circuits *involve using* current, voltage and resistance.

I *remember measuring* the thermal energy last lesson.

You must always use verb + *ing* after prepositions, for example:

You should record the results *after finishing* the experiment.

We learned *about measuring* momentum in the lesson today.

They looked *at increasing* the electrical charge in the circuit.

We calculated the turning effect of forces *by multiplying* the product of the force by the perpendicular distance from the line of action of the force to the pivot or point where the object will turn.

I plan *on studying* atoms next.

They must complete the experiment *without increasing* the pressure.

Past simple

The past simple is used to talk about finished past actions.

Remember the verb *to be* is used to describe somebody or something and can be followed by adjectives and nouns.

	Affirmative	Negative	Question
I	was	was not	Was I...?
You	were	were not	Were you...?
He	was	was not	Was he...?
She	was	was not	Was she...?
It	was	was not	Was it...?
We	were	were not	Were we...?
They	were	were not	Were they...?

Example sentences:

Affirmative	Negative	Question
I *was* a physicist.	I *was not* a physicist.	*Was* I a physicist?
It *was* an electromagnet.	It *was not* an electromagnet.	*Was* it an electromagnet?
They *were* sound waves.	They *were not* sound waves.	*Were* they sound waves?

Regular past verbs

	Affirmative	Negative	Question
I, you, we, they He, she, it	+ verb +*ed*	did not + verb	Did + verb *to be* + verb?

With verbs ending in the letter *e*, just add *d*.

With verbs ending in a consonant (b, c, d, f, g…) + *y*, change the *y* to an *i* and then add *ed* when it follows *he*, *she*, *it*.

For example:

Vowel + *y* = *I stay*, *he stayed*.

Consonant + *y* = *You try*, *it tried*.

	Affirmative	Negative	Question
I, you, he, she, it we, they	I *calculated* the rate. It *created* a vacuum. They *increased* the momentum.	I didn't *calculate* the rate. It didn't *create* a vacuum. They didn't *increase* the momentum.	Did I *calculate* the rate? Did it *create* a vacuum? Did they *increase* the momentum?

Irregular past verbs

Some common verbs have irregular past forms. For example: *become, begin, choose, have, know, make, write*.

	Affirmative	Negative	Question
I, you, he, she, it we, they	It *became* radioactive. He *fell* to Earth. They *lost* electrical charge.	It didn't *become* radioactive. He didn't *fall* to Earth. They didn't *lose* electrical charge.	Did it *become* radioactive? Did he *fall* to Earth? Did they *lose* electrical charge?

The first conditional

The first conditional is used to make predictions and to talk about things that are very likely to happen in certain conditions. It is formed by: *If* + present simple + *will* + verb base form / infinitive without *to*.

If		present simple		subject		will	verb	
If	you	place		iron filings	near a magnet, they	will	form	magnetic field patterns.
If	light waves	hit	an opaque surface	they		will	be blocked	from reaching the other side of that object.

It is possible to start with the *will* clause.

Iron filings *will* form magnetic field patterns if they are placed near a magnet.

Light waves *will* be blocked from reaching the other side of an object if they hit an opaque surface.

The second conditional

The second conditional is used to imagine situations in the present or the future that are very unlikely to happen or are impossible. It is formed by: *if* + past simple + *would* + infinitive.

If		past simple		would	infinitive verb	
If	Earth	had	no moon, it	would	spin	faster.
If	the moon	had	the same gravity as the Earth, it	would	increase	its gravitational force six times and collide with Earth.

It is possible to start with the *would* clause.

The Earth would spin faster if it had no Moon.

The Moon would increase its gravitational force six times and collide with Earth if the Moon had the same gravity as Earth.

Past passive voice

Remember, the passive is used when the person or thing that did the action is unknown, unimportant or not the focus of our interest. We use *by* with the passive if we want to identify who or what did the action.

The past simple passive is formed by using:

was / were + the past participle.

Past active: I used a resistor to provide electrical resistance in a circuit.

Past passive: A resistor was used to provide electrical resistance in a circuit.

Past active: A scientist recorded the volume of water.

Past passive: The volume of water was recorded (by a scientist).

Past active: She used a magnifying lens to observe the object in detail.

Past passive: A magnifying lens was used to observe the object in detail.

Adjectives

Adjectives are words that you can use to describe things, people and places. There are many adjectives in English, some common examples are *small, heavy, average, precious* and *bright*.

Adjectives go before the thing they are describing (adjective + noun) or after the verb *to be* and sense verbs, for example *seems, feels, smells, looks, sounds*. When adjectives modify a pronoun they have to follow the pronoun. For example: *Give me something <u>useful</u>*.

An *enormous* planet.   The planet is *enormous*.

Heavy ion.   The ions are *heavy*.

An *average* velocity.   The velocity is *average*.

There are many synonyms (words that have the same meaning), for example:

Enormous, huge, massive

Heavy, dense, weighty

Average, usual, standard

You can also use adjectives after *how* to create questions, for example:

How far will the ball travel?

How well the experiment goes depends on *how accurate* I am.

How fast will the projectile fly?

Comparative and superlative adjectives

Comparative adjectives are used to compare two nouns. Superlative adjectives are used to compare several things and to express *the most* or *the least*.

Comparative adjectives are formed with *-er* add more. Superlative adjectives are formed with *-est* and *the most*.

Adjectives with one syllable (*big, fast, small, ...*) add *-er*:

Rule	Adjective	Comparative	Superlative
Add *-er* and *-est* to most 1 syllable adjectives	full	fuller	The fullest
	dark	darker	The darkest
	great	greater	The greatest
	loud	louder	The loudest
1 syllable adjectives ending in *e* just add *-r* or *-st*	fine	finer	The finest
	rare	rarer	The rarest
	pale	paler	The palest
	close	closer	The closest
Adjectives ending consonant-vowel-consonant double the final consonant then add *-er* or *-est*	wet	wetter	The wettest
	hot	hotter	The hottest
	flat	flatter	The flattest
	thin	thinner	The thinnest

Rule	Adjective	Comparative	Superlative
1 and 2 syllable adjectives ending vowel + *w* 2 syllable ending vowel + *y* 2 syllable adjectives ending in *le* just add -*er* or -*est*	new low shallow easy gentle	newer lower shallower easier gentler	The newest The lowest The shallowest The easiest The gentlest
1 and 2 syllable adjectives ending consonant + *y* Change the *y* to an *i* then add -*er* or -*est*	rocky noisy empty weighty	rockier noisier emptier weightier	The rockiest The noisiest The emptiest The weightiest
Other 2 syllable adjectives and longer adjectives *More* + adjective or *the most* + adjective	accurate careful common electric	more accurate more careful more common more electric	The most accurate The most careful The most common The most electric
Irregular adjectives	well little far many	better less further more	The best The least The furthest / farthest The most

Use *than* to connect the things being compared:

Solid objects that sink in have a *greater* density *than* water.

Mercury stays *the closest* to Earth *the longest* time.

Venus is *the hottest* planet.

Jupiter has a *lower* average temperature *than* Saturn.

Objects that fall are *weightier than* air.

The *closer* the final result is to the correct value, the *more accurate* the experiment is.

Checking that you have set up an experiment properly is *the best* method to ensure accuracy.

You can compare similar things by using *as* + adjective + *as* or *isn't as* + adjective + *as*.

Venus is *as big as* the Earth.

Jupiter *isn't as hot as* Mercury.

Adverbs

Adverbs show us how an action is done.

Adverbs of manner

Many adverbs of manner are formed by adding -*ly* to the end of adjectives. Adverbs of manner can also answer the question, *how?*

The car's speed increased *quickly*. (It shows how the car's speed increased.)

She drew the graph *accurately*. (It shows how the graph was drawn.)

The gravitational force decreased *slowly*. (It shows how the gravitational force decreased.)

The experiment was conducted *successfully*. (It shows how the experiment was conducted.)

Adverbs of time

Adverbs of time tell you when an action happened and express a point in time. Adverbs of time either go at the beginning or at the end of the clause or sentence.

Initially, we thought the velocity would be greater. / We thought the velocity would be greater, *initially*.

Eventually, the spring snapped. / The spring snapped, *eventually*.

Modal verbs

Modal verbs are auxiliary verbs, for example, *must, shall, will, should, would, can, could, may* and *might*. Modal verbs show necessity, possibility, give advice, warnings or recommendations. They do not change for *I, you, we, they, he, she, it* and they do not use *do / does* in negatives and questions.

Will and *will not* are used to say that you are sure something is going to, or not going to happen.

Will / will not + verb

A spring *will have* maximum potential energy when it is the farthest from its original position.

A weak spring *will not carry* its fair share of the load.

Should and *should not* are used to give advice, warnings or recommendations.

Should / should not + verb

You *should* always *wear* protective eye wear when looking at the Sun.

You *should not look* directly at the Sun.

The examples with *should* in the sentences above are all active. You can also use *should* in the passive form.

Should + *be* + past participle

Protective eye wear should always be worn when looking at the Sun.

Can is used to talk about ability and possibility. It is formed by adding a verb after *can* and *may*. *Cannot* shows the lack of ability and possibility and *may not* shows the lack of possibility.

Can for ability

Dogs *can* hear sound frequencies as high as 65,000 Hz.

Owls are nocturnal and they *can* see in the dark.

Can and *may* for possibility

Electricity *can/may* pass through wood, but it's not a good conductor.

Light *cannot* pass easily through translucent objects.

You can also use the modal verb *can* and *may* in the passive form. It is formed like this: *Can* + *be* + past participle or *may* + *be* + past participle

For example:

Wood *can be transformed* into a better conductor by wetting it.

Light *can be stopped* from passing through surfaces by making the surfaces opaque.

High sound frequencies *can be heard* by dogs.

Objects *can be seen* by owls in the dark.

Connectives

Connectives are words or phrases that act like glue and join two parts of a sentence together. There are many connectives in English, and it is important to choose the right ones for each sentence because they work differently and can change the meaning of sentences.

Connectives for cause and consequence

To express a cause + a consequence, *therefore* and *consequently* are used to express the consequence. For example:

Cause	Connective	Consequence
There was a temperature difference between them,	therefore,	energy transferred from a hotter place to a colder place.

OR

Cause	Connective	Consequence
There was a temperature difference between them,	consequently	energy transferred from a hotter place to a colder place.

Therefore generally goes before the second piece of information. When you use *therefore*, you need a comma after it.

Expressing differences: *but, although, whereas, while, however, in contrast, on the other hand*

You can express the difference between things by using *but, although, whereas, while, however, in contrast* and *on the other hand.*

A force exerted on an object changes the object's speed, direction of movement or shape, *whereas* pressure is a measure of how much force is acting upon an area.

Although distance and displacement appear to be similar, they are different.

Distance describes how much space an object has travelled during movement, *but* displacement refers the object's overall change in position.

The highest surface part of a sound wave is called the crest, *while* the lowest part is known as the trough.

Speed is the time rate at which an object is moving along a path, *however* velocity is the rate and direction of an object's movement.

If matter contains more protons than electrons, it is positively charged. *In contrast*, if there are more electrons than protons, it is negatively charged.

If matter contains more protons than electrons, it is positively charged. *On the other hand,* if there are more electrons than protons, it is negatively charged.

Expressing reasons and cause: *because and since*

Because and *since* can both be used to introduce a cause. When using because and since, either goes in front of the cause or in the middle, for example:

Because of gravity, we fall down, not up.

We fall down, not up *because* of gravity.

Since there is oxygen and water, humans can exist on planet Earth.

Humans can exist on planet Earth *since* there is oxygen and water.

So, can be used to talk about effects or consequences; *so*, goes in front of the effect:

There is gravity on Earth, *so* we fall down, not up.

There is oxygen and water on planet Earth, *so* humans can exist.

Connectives that express examples include: *for example*, *for instance* and *such as*.

There are many types of energy, *for example*, electrical, sound and light.

Gas pressure occurs when gas particles hit the walls of their container. *For instance*, the collisions caused by gas inside a balloon cause forces to travel outwards in all directions; this gives the balloon its shape.

Atoms are made of tiny particles, *such as* protons, neutrons and electrons.

Because answers the question: *why?*

Many hollow objects float on water *because* they have air inside them, this increases the volume and the upwards push of the object.

Connect two actions that happen at the same time together using *as*

You can use *as* to connect two actions that happen at the same time. *As* can be placed at the beginning of the sentence or between the two actions. If you start the sentence with *as*, you need a comma between the two actions.

As the balloon inflates, the pressure inside the balloon increases.

The pressure inside the balloon increases *as* the balloon inflates.

As you go higher into the atmosphere, the air becomes thinner.

The air becomes thinner *as* you go higher into the atmosphere.

As the air becomes thinner, the atmospheric pressure drops.

The atmospheric pressure drops *as* the air becomes thinner.

Definite and indefinite articles

The indefinite article is *a* or *an,* and are used to talk about singular nouns. Indefinite articles are used to talk about general or non-specific nouns. *A* is used before words that start with a consonant, for example, *a* force, and *an* is used before words that start with a vowel, for example, *an* insulator. The definite article is *the* and it can be used to talk about singular or plural nouns. The definite article *the* is used to refer to particular nouns or when only one exists, for example *the* moon. *The* can also be used when the identity of the noun is known to the reader, for example, the second time something is mentioned.

A and *an*

A circuit.

An electrical circuit.

I have built *an* electrical circuit. *The* circuit transmits electric current to sound a buzzer. *The* buzzer stops when I press *a* switch.

The

The magnet (singular noun)   *The* magnets (plural noun)   *The* radiation (uncountable noun)

The for unique things

The Moon   *The* Earth   *The* Sun

The is also used before superlative adjectives.

The shortest soundwave.

The loudest sound.

The most powerful force.

Prefixes

Prefixes are a letter or a group of letters added to the beginning of words to change the meaning of the root word. A root word is the basic form of the word, in its shortest form.

Prefix	Meaning	Example
sub	under / smaller	submerge / subdivide / subscript
super	above	superscript

To *submerge* is to keep something under the surface of liquid.

Imperatives

Imperatives are used to give instructions, commands and orders. Imperative sentences start with a verb.

Use an ammeter to measure electric current in ampere.

Calculate the forces produced.

Put insulation around the wires.

Connect the two wires together.

Sequencing

It is important to know what order to do things in a practical experiment. You can use words and phrases like, *first* or *first of all*, *then*, *next*, *after that* and *finally* to show the sequence of instructions.

First, attach the two clamps to the clamp stand *then* position the clamp stand near the edge of the bench. *After that*, hang the spring from the top clamp. *Next*, attach the ruler to the bottom clamp vertically then hook the weight onto the bottom of the spring. *Finally*, take a reading on the ruler.

You can also use *before* and *after* to express the order of events.

Before the light illuminates, the switch closes the circuit.

After the switch closes, the light illuminates.

As can be used to talk about two things that happen at the same time. Use *as + verb*

For example:

As water freezes, heat energy is released.

As the temperature of an object decreases, the average kinetic energy of its particles decreases.

Prepositions

When you want to describe an action, you can use the preposition *to* before actions and *for* before people.

When you want to describe an action, you can use this pattern:

It is + adjective + *to* + verb

For example:

It is easy to measure distance, as distance is speed multiplied by time.

It is difficult to remember some theories in physics.

It is important to conserve energy.

If you want to add a person, add *for* + (person) after the adjective.

For example:

It is common for students to get refraction angles wrong.

It is helpful for scientists to record their findings.

It is important for physicists to have a good understanding of maths.

Prepositions can also be used to show position and motion. Some examples are: *between, beyond, towards, to, up, down, away from, in front of, around.*

Sentences are formed by: preposition + noun or pronoun

Preposition	Meaning	Example
Between	In the middle with something on each side	Jupiter is *between* the Earth and Uranus.
Beyond	Further away from	Pluto is far *beyond* Mars.
Towards	Closer to	If you jump out of a plane, you fall *towards* Earth because of the force of gravity.
From	The place at which a motion or action starts	Equipment in space that travels around the Earth, passes television, radio, and telephone signals *from* one place to another.
Away from	At a greater distance from its original position	Planet Earth is slowly moving *away from* the sun.
Into	To enter a space	When a meteoroid travels *into* the Earth's upper atmosphere, it heats up due to friction from the air.
Out of	To leave a space	An airplane cannot fly *out of* the Earth's atmosphere, because jet engines use oxygen from the air to function.

The proposition *by* shows who did the action or how an outcome was achieved.

For example:

The research was conducted *by* top physicians at the university.

Ferromagnetic materials are strongly attracted *by* magnetic fields.

Pronouns

Pronouns are words that can replace nouns and refer to someone or something mentioned before, and it is clear what or who you are talking about. The pronouns *they, it, them, their* and *its* are used frequently in science, and they help you to avoid having to repeat nouns.

For example:

The rings of Saturn are the most extensive in the Solar System. *They* consist of many small particles. *Its* rings range in size from micrometers to meters.

Saturn is the sixth planet from the Sun and *it* has 82 moons. Fifty-three of *them* are confirmed and named and another 29 moons are awaiting confirmation of discovery and official naming. *Their* shape helps to provide and collect material from Saturn's rings.

They = rings   Its = Saturn's   it = Saturn   them = moons   their = the moons'

Relative pronouns

Relative pronouns connect a clause or phrase to a noun or pronoun. The clause describes the noun. Common relative pronouns are *who*, *where*, *when* and *that*.

Relative pronoun	Usage
Who	People
Where	Places

Relative pronoun	Usage
That	Things
When	Moments in time

For example:

We read about the physicist *who* discovered X rays.

I visited the place *where* Isaac Newton discovered gravity.

The instructions show the process *that* we must follow.

I remember the time *when* I first experienced static electricity.

Talking about similarities between two things

You can use *both, neither, all* and *no* to talk about similarities between two things or people. Use *both* and *neither,* with countable nouns and *all* and *no* with uncountable nouns.

You can also use pronouns to replace nouns after *both, neither, all, no.*

For example:

Both inner and outer planets revolve around the sun.

Both of *them* revolve around the sun.

Neither Mercury *nor* Venus have any moons.

Neither of *them* have any moons.

No oxygen is produced on any planet, except the Earth.

No oxygen is produced on any of *them*, except the Earth.

All light is reflected from other planets.

All light is reflected from *them*.

Open and closed questions

There are two types of questions in English, open and closed. Closed questions usually start with *can, does, is, will,* and can only be answered with *yes* or *no*. Open questions are sometimes called Wh- questions, because most of the questions start with wh-, for example, *where, when, what, who.*

Examples of closed questions:

Can you explain the theory of relativity? (answer – yes or no)

Does light bend around corners? (answer – yes or no)

Is copper a good conductor of electricity? (answer – yes or no)

Will heavy objects fall faster than light objects? (answer – yes or no)

Examples of open questions:

Where on Earth is gravity the strongest?

When was the battery invented?

What is magnitude in physics?

Who invented the transistor?

Chapter 1

Making measurements

IN THIS CHAPTER YOU WILL:

Science skills:

- describe how to take measurements of length, volume and time

- describe what density is and whether an object will float.

English skills:

- describe experiments and give instructions using sequencers with imperatives and the past passive voice

- use adjectives, comparatives and superlatives.

Exercise 1.1 Measuring length and volume

IN THIS EXERCISE YOU WILL:

Science skills:

- understand some of the important terms used when taking measurements in physics.

English skills:

- use the correct verb forms and words like *first*, *then*, and *finally* to give instructions and write descriptions.

KEY WORDS

volume: the space occupied by an object

SI unit: the Système International d'Unités is the internationally agreed system of units for scientists all over the world

immerse: to cover something in a fluid (usually water) so that the object is submerged

In this exercise, you are going to look at some of the important terms used when taking measurements of quantities, such as length and **volume**, as well as how to give instructions.

1 a Read the paragraph below and then complete the table with words from
the paragraph.

> Jake measured the length of a block of wood. He used a ruler to
> measure it. He wrote the following statement in his notebook:
>
> length of block = 22.4 cm

Term	Definition	Example from paragraph
quantity	something that can be measured	
measuring instrument	what is used to measure a quantity	
value	the result of measuring a quantity	

b The value of a quantity has a number and a unit. What is the unit of length
in the paragraph in part **a**?

....

> **LANGUAGE TIP**
>
> Each unit has a symbol, for example, kilogram (kg), metre (m) and cubic metre (m^3).

2 a Complete the first two columns of the table using the words below.
Then write the **SI unit** for each quantity in the third column.

balance   length   mass   measuring cylinder
metre ruler   stopwatch   time   volume

Measuring instrument	Quantity measured	SI unit

b Write each row of the table as an instruction. One has been done for you.
Use the Language tip to help you.

Use a metre ruler to measure length in centimetres. ....

....

....

> **LANGUAGE TIP**
>
> To give instructions, use the basic form of a verb, for example: *stand, hold, cut, observe.* This is called the imperative and goes at the start of the sentence:
>
> *Use* a ruler to measure length.

LANGUAGE FOCUS

When you give instructions, use words like *first, next, then, after that* and *finally* to help the reader follow the steps.

Use *first* to begin your instructions:

First, put an empty beaker on the balance and take a reading.

Use *next, then* or *after that* to introduce each following step. (In this context, they mean the same thing.)

Then/Next/After that, fill the beaker with water, place the beaker on the balance and take a second reading.

Use *finally* to introduce the last step:

Finally, subtract the first reading from the second reading to find the mass of the water.

To give instructions, you only need the basic verb (the imperative). To describe an experiment, use the past tense. For most verbs, this means adding *-ed* to the base verb. For irregular verbs, look at a verb list. These lists give three forms of the verb:

give, gave, given

hold, held, held

The second form is the past form: *gave, held*

---

3 **a** Read Siti's description of how she measured the volume of a stone and underline the verbs in the past tense.

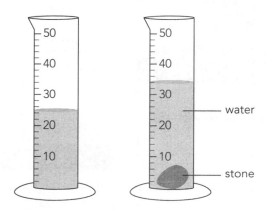

Figure 1.1: Apparatus to find the volume of a stone.

I half-filled a measuring cylinder with water. I recorded the volume of the water. I **immersed** a stone under the water and recorded the new volume. To determine the volume of the stone, I calculated the difference between the two volumes.

b Read the Language focus box again, then write Siti's description as instructions. The first step has been done for you.

First, half-fill the measuring cylinder with water.

....

....

....

Exercise 1.2 Density

IN THIS EXERCISE YOU WILL:

Science skill:

• describe density and understand whether an object will float or not.

English skill:

• describe and compare things using adjectives.

KEY WORDS

density: the ratio of mass per unit volume for a substance

mass: the quantity of matter in an object

In this exercise you are going to look at **density**, which is the measure of a substance's **mass** per unit volume, and whether or not an object will float.

4 a (Circle) the correct equation for calculating density.

$$\text{density} = \text{mass} \times \text{volume} \qquad \text{density} = \frac{\text{volume}}{\text{mass}} \qquad \text{density} = \frac{\text{mass}}{\text{volume}}$$

b If mass is measured in kilograms and volume is measured in cubic metres, give the unit of density.

....

> **LANGUAGE TIP**
>
> The word *per* means *for each* and is often shown by a solidus (/).

LANGUAGE FOCUS

Adjectives are words that describe things, for example: *dense, heavy, complex, narrow, scientific, small*.

Adjectives come before nouns or after *to be*, and they only have one form. This means you use the same adjective for singulars and plurals:

A complex experiment   Complex questions   The questions were complex.

Use the comparative form of adjectives to compare two things.

To make the comparative form of adjectives with one syllable (for example, *small*) or with two syllables ending in -y or -w (for example, *heavy, narrow*), add -er:

smaller   heavier   narrower   (Note: final -y becomes *i*.)

To make the comparative form of other adjectives, put *more* in front of them:

more complex

Then add *than*:

Those words are more complex <u>than</u> these words.

To compare more than two things, use the superlative form of the adjective.

-er comparatives → *the -est* superlatives

more comparatives → *the most* superlatives

For example:

This ball was <u>heavier</u> than the other balls. It was <u>the heaviest</u> of all of the balls.

This experiment was more <u>complex</u> than the other experiments. It was the <u>most complex</u> of all of them.

5   The adjectives in the table are frequently used in physics. Complete the table with their comparative and superlative forms. Use the Language focus box to help you.

Adjective	Comparative form	Superlative form
large		
high		
great		
heavy		
accurate		

6 Complete the paragraph about density and floating using comparative and superlative forms of the adjectives in brackets.

Density depends on mass and volume. If two objects have the same volume

but one object has a .... [great] mass, this means it will have a

.... [large] density. If an object is less dense than water then it will

float. If an object is .... [dense] than water then it will sink. If you

pour three liquids with different densities into a measuring cylinder, then the liquid

with .... [high] density will sink to the bottom of the measuring

cylinder. The liquid with .... [low] density will be at the top.

Exercise 1.3 Measuring time

IN THIS EXERCISE YOU WILL:

Science skill:

* describe how to measure time.

English skill:

* use the past passive to describe an experiment.

KEY WORDS

fiducial marker: a mark used to identify the number of rotations

period: the time taken for one complete wave to pass a particular point

In this exercise, you are going to look at measuring time. In physics, time is often measured using a stopwatch or a light gate with an electronic timer.

7 Complete the sentences about measuring time using the words below.

average   interval   oscillation   period   stopwatch   time

When you want to measure a short .... of time, such as the

.... of a pendulum, you use a .... to measure several

oscillations then divide the .... by the number of oscillations to

calculate the .... time of one oscillation. The time for one oscillation

is called the ....

8 **a** Ajay carried out an experiment to measure the **period** of rotation of a potter's wheel. His teacher gave him the following instructions:

- Use a **fiducial marker** to mark the edge of the wheel.

- Switch on the wheel.

- Start the stopwatch.

- Time how long it takes for 20 rotations.

- Find the time it takes for one rotation (the period).

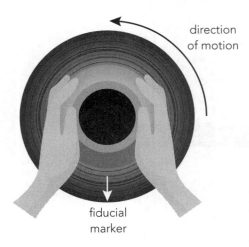

direction of motion

fiducial marker

Figure 1.2: A potter's wheel.

Use the instructions to write a description of the experiment using the past tense. Use sequencers in your answer. The first sentence has been done for you.

First, Ajay used a fiducial marker to mark the edge of the wheel.

....

....

....

LANGUAGE FOCUS

When you write about experiments, you often need to use the past passive. This is because often, in science, the action is more important than the person doing the action. You can also use the passive when you do not know who did the action.

A scientist recorded the volume of water.   (past tense)

Is it important to know which scientist? If the answer is no, the following sentence is better:

The volume of water was recorded.   (past passive)

To change a past active sentence into a past passive sentence:

Look for the object (the thing after the verb) and move it to the front of the sentence.

The volume of water…

Decide if the word at the front (*volume*) is singular or plural, then add *was* (for singular) or *were* (for plural). *Was* and *were* are the past forms of *to be*:

The volume of water was…

Determine the past participle of the main verb (*recorded*). With regular verbs, add *-ed* to the verb (*record → recorded*). With irregular verbs, you need a verb table. The past participle is in the third column. For example:

bring	*brought*	*brought*
give	*gave*	*given*
make	*made*	*made*
put	*put*	*put*

Finally, add the past participle to the sentence:

The volume of water was <u>recorded</u>.

Here is another example:

We took the measurements using a measuring cylinder.

The measurements were taken using a measuring cylinder.

b Rewrite the description that you wrote in part **a** using the past passive. The first sentence has been done for you.

First, a fiducial marker was used to mark the edge of the wheel.

....

....

....

> Chapter 2
Describing motion

IN THIS CHAPTER YOU WILL:

Science skills:

- describe the speed of an object and understand that acceleration is a change in speed

- analyse and interpret distance–time and speed–time graphs.

English skills:

- understand and use the vocabulary related to the motion of an object

- use the correct scientific terms and the present simple tense to describe and analyse distance–time and speed–time graphs.

Exercise 2.1 Speed

IN THIS EXERCISE YOU WILL:

Science skills:

- describe the speed of an object and how to calculate it.

English skills:

- understand and use important terms for describing speed.

KEY WORDS

speed: the distance travelled by an object per unit of time

average speed: the speed calculated from total distance travelled divided by total time taken

instantaneous speed: the speed at a particular moment in time

In this exercise, you are going to look at the **speed** of an object and important terms used to describe it.

1 Find the seven words in the word string. Write them on the lines below. One has been done for you.

speeddistancetimeaveragemetresecondinstantaneous

speed

....

....

....

....

....

> **LANGUAGE TIP**
>
> Definitions often follow this pattern: [X] *is a/the* [Y] *that +* verb:
>
> *A stopwatch is an instrument that measures time.*

2 Complete the sentences about speed. Use the words and phrases below.

average speed   instantaneous speed   metres

metres per second   seconds

a $\dfrac{\text{total distance travelled}}{\text{total time taken}}$ is the equation that is used to calculate

....

b When you divide distance (in ....) by time

(in ....) that gives you the SI unit for speed: ....

c The equation that is used to calculate the .... of an object

(its speed at a particular moment in time) is $v = \dfrac{s}{t}$.

3 a A car travels 250 metres in 20 seconds. Calculate the speed of the car. Give the unit.

Speed: ....

b Explain whether this is the **average speed** or the **instantaneous speed**.

....

....

Exercise 2.2 Distance–time graphs

IN THIS EXERCISE YOU WILL:

Science skills:

- describe and interpret distance–time graphs.

English skills:

- use key terms and the present simple for describing and interpreting distance–time graphs.

KEY WORDS

distance–time graph: a graph showing the motion of an object with time on the *x*-axis and distance on the *y*-axis

gradient: the slope of a line on a graph

In this exercise, you are going to look at **distance–time graphs**. The **gradient** of the graph tells you how fast the object is travelling. A steeper slope means a greater speed.

LANGUAGE FOCUS

In physics, there are scientific words that help you to talk about, or analyse, graphs. Some of the words are nouns, including:

axes (plural) *x-axis* *y-axis* *origin* *point* *line* *curve* *gradient*

Others are verbs:

increase *decrease* *level off* *intersect* *reach* *show*

And others are adjectives and adverbs:

Adjectives: *steep* *stable* *constant* *varying* *gradual* *steady* *faster* *slower* *horizontal*

Adverbs: *sharply* *gradually*

An adverb is a word that describes a verb. In English, most adverbs are made by adding *-ly* to an adjective.

a <u>gradual</u> rise (describing a noun)

The car speeds up <u>gradually</u>. (describing a verb)

It is a good idea to collect graphs and practise labelling them. The more you use these words, the quicker you will learn them.

LANGUAGE TIP

Speed up and *slow down* do not express movement up or down. They mean *get faster* (speed up) and *get slower* (slow down).

4   Label the parts of the distance–time graph using the words and phrases below:

faster constant speed   **gradient**   **origin**

slower constant speed   **x-axis**   **y-axis**   **zero speed**

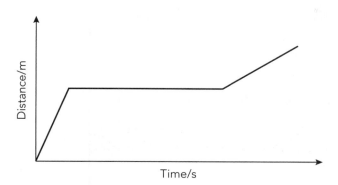

Figure 2.1: A distance–time graph.

5   Figure 2.2 shows the distance–time graph for a car.

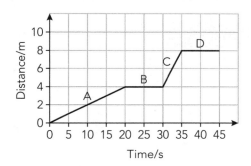

Figure 2.2: A distance–time graph for a car.

Fill in the gaps to complete the sentences about the distance–time graph using the words below. Not all the words are needed.

constant   faster   gradient   horizontal   slower   stationary

a   The speed of the car is shown by the .... of the distance–
time graph.

b   Section A is a straight line, which shows that the car is travelling at
.... speed.

c   The car moves .... during section A than during section C.

d   Sections B and D have .... lines, which show that the car is
....

LANGUAGE FOCUS

In physics, the most common way to describe what you see is to use a tense called the present simple.

Decide what verb you want to use. For example: *show, go, intersect, increase*.

If the subject is *I, you, we, they* or a plural noun, you do not need to change the verb:

You use these words to describe graphs.

The lines intersect.

If the subject is *it, he, she* or a singular noun, add *-s*. Verbs ending *-s, -z, -ch, -sh* or *-o* need *-es*:

The line goes through point Z.

The car passes the measuring device.

Nearly all other verbs only need *-s*:

The vehicle accelerates.

The ball drops.

6   a   Figure 2.3 shows the distance–time graph for a toy car. Describe the motion of the car during each section of the graph using the present simple tense.

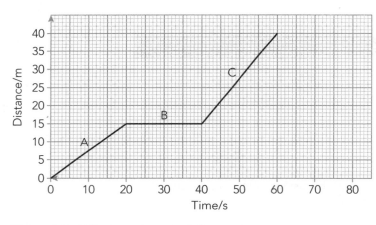

Figure 2.3: A distance–time graph for a toy car.

....

....

....

....

b i How far does the toy car travel during section A?

....

ii How far does the toy car travel during section C?

....

c Calculate the speed of the toy car in section A and section C.

Section A: .... m/s

Section C: .... m/s

Exercise 2.3 Acceleration and speed–time graphs

IN THIS EXERCISE YOU WILL:

Science skills:

- describe acceleration as the change in speed of an object

- analyse and interpret speed–time graphs.

English skills:

- understand and use a variety of terms to describe motion

- use the present simple to describe speed–time graphs.

KEY WORDS

speed–time graph: a graph showing the motion of an object with time on the x-axis and speed on the y-axis

acceleration: the rate of change of an object's speed

deceleration: slowing down; a negative acceleration

In this exercise, you are going to look at **speed–time graphs**. The gradient of the graph tells you the **acceleration** of the object. A steeper slope means a greater acceleration.

7 Complete the table by putting a tick (✓) in the correct column to show whether the object is accelerating, at constant speed or **decelerating**. The first one has been done for you.

Description	Constant speed	Accelerating	Decelerating
The speed of the cricket ball is 25 m/s throughout the journey.	✓		
The bike slows down near the corner.			
The ball moves at 30 m/s on the flat surface.			
As the toy car rolls downhill, it speeds up.			
The ball gradually comes to a stop at the bottom.			
A bus changes its speed from 30 km/h to 50 km/h.			

LANGUAGE FOCUS

In physics, you need to understand and use a variety of words to describe motion. The words include different ways of saying *go up*, *go down* and *stay the same*:

Verbs:

Go up: *rise, increase, climb* (of speed), *speed up*

Go down: *fall, decrease, drop* (of speed), *slow down*

Stay the same: *remain the same, not change* (of speed), *remain constant*

Adjectives:

gradual, steady, constant, sharp, rapid, quick, sudden, fast, slow

Remember that you can form the adverb of these adjectives by adding *-ly*. In the case of *steady*, the adverb is *steadily*. (Note: the adverb of *fast* is also *fast*.)

Other terms:

(travel/move) at a steady speed, (travel/move) at (25) m/s, a sudden increase (in), a sharp drop (in), a sharp rise (in), a gradual rise/fall (in), come to a (sudden) halt/stop, a change in (speed/direction)

8 Abu gets in his car to drive to work. Complete the sentences about Abu's car journey using expressions from the Language focus box.

  a When Abu starts the car and presses the accelerator, the car speeds

  .... gradually.

  b The car travels .... along the road.

  c When Abu reaches some red traffic lights, he presses the brake sharply and the car

  ....

9 Look at the speed–time graph in Figure 2.4.

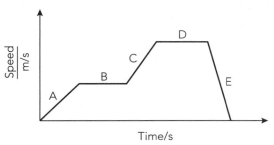

Figure 2.4: A speed–time graph.

  a Which sections show the object travelling at a constant speed?

  ....

  b **i** Which sections show the object accelerating (speeding up)?

  ....

  ii Which section shows the greatest acceleration?

  ....

  c Which section shows the object decelerating (slowing down)

  ....

10 a Figure 2.5 shows the speed–time graph for a car. Describe the motion of the car in each section of the journey using the present simple tense and the correct terms.

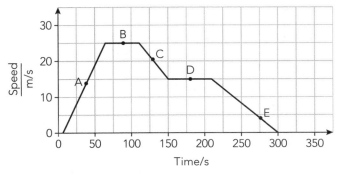

Figure 2.5: Speed–time graph for a car.

....

....

....

....

b　Which section shows the greatest **deceleration**? Explain why it shows this.

....

....

....

....

> # Chapter 3
Forces and motion

IN THIS CHAPTER YOU WILL:

Science skills:

- describe types of force and how a resultant force can change the motion of an object
- describe mass, weight and gravitational field strength.

English skills:

- practise using *-ing* forms and relative clauses to describe and define nouns
- use expressions to explain the relationships between variables.

Exercise 3.1 Forces

IN THIS EXERCISE YOU WILL:

Science skills:

- describe types of force and how a resultant force can change the motion of an object.

English skills:

- use *-ing* forms in descriptions.

KEY WORDS

force: the action of one body on a second body

resultant force: the single force that has the same effect on a body as two or more forces

contact force: the force between two objects that are touching

In this exercise, you are going to look at different **forces** and the effect of a **resultant force** on an object.

1   a   Find the seven terms to do with forces in the word string. Write them on the
lines below. One has been done for you.

weightcontactfrictionairresistancenewtonupthrustdrag

weight
....

....

....

....

....

....

LANGUAGE FOCUS

To describe what you can see, hear, smell, etc., you often want to give the
thing or person and the action it is doing. The easiest way is to add verb +
-*ing* after the thing or person:

I smell <u>paper burning</u>.

I hear a <u>phone ringing</u>.

If the verb you want to use is short and ends with consonant-vowel-consonant,
you need to double the last consonant:

cut   *I hear someone cu<u>tt</u>ing down a tree.*

run   *I observed a child ru<u>nn</u>ing.*

If the verb ends with -*e*, remove the e before you add -*ing*:

decreas<u>e</u>   *We noticed the speed decreas<u>ing</u>.*

mov<u>e</u>   *We saw the iron filings mov<u>ing</u>.*

---

2   Complete the sentences with the correct -*ing* form of the verbs given below.

acting   falling   floating   moving   rubbing

a   Solid friction occurs when two surfaces are .... together and it
can produce heat.

b   Drag is a type of friction caused by an object ....
through water.

c   The **contact force** stops you .... through the ground.

d   Upthrust explains why the swimmers are .... in the
swimming pool.

e   A resultant force .... on an object can make the object change
speed or direction.

3   Sanjay has made a toy boat and puts it in water. Figure 3.1 shows two forces
acting on the boat, causing it to sink.

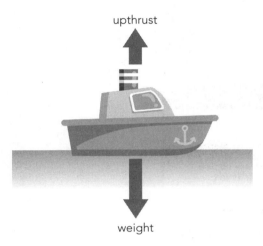

Figure 3.1: Two forces acting on a toy boat.

a   What does the length of a force arrow indicate?

....

b   The upthrust is 75 N and the weight is 83 N.

i   State whether the forces on the toy boat are balanced.

....

ii   Calculate the resultant force acting on the boat and give its direction.

....

Exercise 3.2 Mass and weight

IN THIS EXERCISE YOU WILL:

Science skills:

- describe the differences between mass and weight.

English skills:

- practise writing definitions using relative pronouns.

KEY WORDS

mass: how much matter an object contains

weight: the force of gravity that acts on the object

acceleration of free fall: the increase in speed of an object falling freely under gravity

In this exercise, you are going to look at the differences between the **mass** and **weight** of an object.

4   Read the statements in the table below. Decide whether each statement refers to mass or weight then tick (✓) the correct box. One has been done for you.

Statement	Mass	Weight
It is a force.		✓
It is the amount of matter that an object contains.		
It is measured in newtons.		
It is the pull of the Earth's gravity on an object.		
It is measured in kilograms.		
It can be represented by an arrow and has a direction.		

5   Fill in the spaces to complete the paragraph about mass and weight.

Mass is measured in .... while weight is measured in

.... If you take an object to the Moon, its .... will

stay the same but its .... will change.

LANGUAGE FOCUS

In science, you often read or write definitions of words or terms. A definition explains what a thing is or who a person is. It answers the questions: *What is…? Who is…? or What does… mean?*

Definitions are usually written in the present simple or the past simple, and often start with: subject + *is/was + a/the … + who/that…*

When you define a person, it is better to use *who* than *that*:

Newton <u>was the</u> physicist <u>who</u> devised the three laws of motion.

When you define a thing or a process, use *that*:

Newton's first law <u>is a</u> law <u>that</u> is known as the law of inertia.

6   a   (Circle) the correct option to complete each sentence.

   i   Weight is the name given to the force on an object near the Earth's surface *who / that* is caused by the Earth's gravity.

   ii   Gravity is the force *that / who* pulls an object towards the Earth.

   iii   Galileo Galilei was an Italian physicist *who / that* showed that **acceleration of free fall** is the approximately the same for all objects near the Earth's surface.

   b   Rewrite the sentences as one sentence using *who* or *that*.

   i   A physicist is a scientist. A physicist specialises in physics.

   ....

   ....

   ii   Gravity is a force. Gravity exists between two objects with mass.

   ....

   ....

   iii   Weight is the gravitational force acting on all objects. Weight varies on different planets because they have different forces of gravity.

   ....

   ....

   iv   All falling objects have the same acceleration near the Earth's surface. It is known as the acceleration of free fall and is $9.8 \, \text{m/s}^2$.

   ....

   ....

Exercise 3.3 Gravitational field strength

IN THIS EXERCISE YOU WILL:

Science skills:

- describe gravitational field strength and use it to calculate weight.

English skills:

- use expressions to explain the relationships between variables.

KEY WORDS

gravitational field strength: the gravitational force exerted per unit mass placed at that point

variable: a quantity that can be different values

In this exercise, you will look at **gravitational field strength** and learn useful expressions to explain the relationships between **variables**.

7 Complete the table about units.

Quantity	Unit
mass	
weight	
acceleration of free fall	
gravitational field strength	

LANGUAGE FOCUS

In physics, you often need to talk about the relationship between variables. You may know the expression *the same as*, but here are four more useful expressions:

constant   *directly proportional to*   *inversely proportional to*   *equal to*

constant: there is no change

directly proportional to: an increase (or decrease) in one variable results in an increase (or decrease) in another variable; the two variables change at the same rate and the graph is a straight line that goes through the origin

inversely proportional to: an increase in one variable results in a decrease in another variable; the rate of change of one variable is the reciprocal of the rate of change of the other variable

equal to: the same as

8   Complete the sentences using the words and phrases below. Not all the words are needed.

**constant   directly proportional to   equal to
inversely proportional to**

a   The mass of a person on Mars is .... their mass on Jupiter.

b   The weight of an object is .... its mass.

c   The gravitational field strength of the Earth is equivalent to the acceleration of

free fall and is approximately .... near the surface of the Earth.

9   An astronaut has a mass of 80 kg and travels to different planets. The table shows the gravitational field strength on the different planets.

a   (Circle) the equation used to calculate gravitational field strength.

$$g = \frac{m}{W} \qquad g = mW \qquad g = \frac{W}{m}$$

b   Calculate the weight of the astronaut on each planet and complete the table.

Planet	Gravitational field strength N/kg	Weight of astronaut/N
Earth	9.8	
Mars	3.7	
Jupiter	24.7	
Venus	8.8	
Saturn	10.5	

Chapter 4
Turning effects

IN THIS CHAPTER YOU WILL:

Science skills:

- describe moments and the principle of moments
- describe the conditions for equilibrium and how centre of gravity affects stability.

English skills:

- use prepositions when describing moments
- use connectives and comparative adjectives to describe moments and stability.

Exercise 4.1 Moments

IN THIS EXERCISE YOU WILL:

Science skills:

- describe the moment of a force and applications of moments.

English skills:

- identify and use prepositions when describing moments.

KEY WORDS

moment: the turning effect of a force about a pivot

pivot: the fixed point about which a lever turns

anticlockwise: turning in the opposite direction from the hands on a clock

In this exercise, you are going to look at **moments**. We use the effects of moments in many real-life situations, such as opening a paint can with a screwdriver, using scissors and lifting a wheelbarrow.

1   Complete the sentences using the words below. Words may be used more than once.

        balanced   **moment**   **turning effect**   **unbalanced**

a   The .... of a force is defined as the product of a force and the perpendicular distance from the **pivot**.

b   The moment is a measure of the .... of the force that causes an object to rotate.

c   A see-saw is balanced when the .... on one side of the pivot is equal to the .... on the other side.

d   If additional weight is added on one side of the see-saw, the see-saw becomes ....

LANGUAGE TIP

Additional is a useful adjective that means *extra*, or *more than before*.

For example: *We needed additional data to complete the experiment.*

LANGUAGE FOCUS

In physics, when you talk about ideas such as forces and moments, you often need to use prepositions. Prepositions are words that go in front of nouns (e.g. *table*), pronouns (e.g. *it*) and *-ing* verb forms (e.g. *observing*) and they can help you express location and movement. Here, we will look at prepositions with nouns and pronouns.

There are many prepositions in English, including *at*, *to*, *on*, *in* and *under*, but four are particularly useful:

About   against   at   to

About often expresses movement around something:

He walked about the room, spinning a pen around his finger.

Against often expresses movement or force in the opposite direction:

It is difficult to swim against the current in a river.

At does not express movement. It suggests something is not moving:

He stood at the table. (He was not moving.)

To expresses movement that ends at the point given after *to*. It is also used with *close*:

He walked to the door. (He stopped at the door).

The glass was placed close to the edge.

2 Figure 4.1a shows a person using a wrench. Figure 4.1b shows two people on a balanced see-saw. Look at the pictures and circle the correct preposition in each sentence.

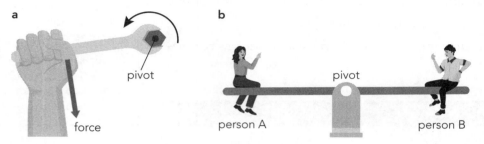

Figure 4.1: a A person using a wrench; **b** Two people on a see-saw.

a When the person applies a force *against / about / to* the handle of the wrench, the wrench moves in an **anticlockwise** direction.

b The moment of person A is equal to the moment of person B *against / about / to* the pivot.

c If the person holds the wrench closer *against / about / to* the pivot, they will need to apply a greater force to turn the wrench.

d If person A moves towards the pivot, they will exert less force *against / about / to* person B and their moment about the pivot will be less.

e The person needs less force to turn a wrench with a long handle *against / about / to* the pivot than a wrench with a short handle.

3 Figure 4.2 shows a balance crane. Fill in the spaces to complete the paragraph about how it works using *about, against, at* and *to*.

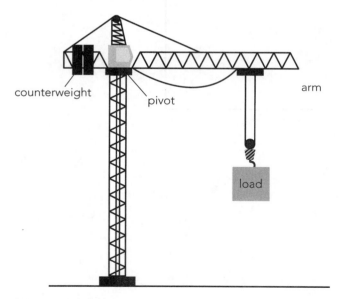

Figure 4.2: A balance crane.

A balance crane is a machine that can lift heavy objects. The arm of the crane is balanced .... the pivot. The moment of the weight of the counterweight is balanced .... the moment of the weight of the load. The load and the counterweight can be moved along the arm nearer .... or away from the pivot. To lift a smaller load, the load is moved closer .... the pivot so that there are equal turning forces .... the pivot.

Exercise 4.2 Equilibrium

IN THIS EXERCISE YOU WILL:

Science skills:

- describe the conditions for equilibrium
- use the principle of moments in calculations.

English skills:

- use connectives of contrast: *but, whereas* and *although*.

KEY WORDS

equilibrium: when no net force and no net moment act on an object

principle of moments: when an object is in equilibrium, the sum of anticlockwise moments about any point equals the sum of clockwise moments about the same point

clockwise: turning in the same direction as the hands on a clock

In this exercise, you will look at objects in **equilibrium** and how the **principle of moments** can be used in calculations.

4   Fill in the spaces to complete the paragraph about a see-saw. Use the words below.

> **anticlockwise   equilibrium   forces   moment**
> **pivot   turning effects**

For a see-saw to be in ...., the .... on it need to be balanced. The .... of the forces on each side of the see-saw also need to be balanced. When the see-saw is balanced, the **clockwise** .... is equal to the .... moment about the ....

LANGUAGE FOCUS

When you want to contrast two facts or conditions in a sentence, you can connect them using connectives. For example, *but*:

See-saw A is balanced, but see-saw B is not.

In science, you often find different connectives of contrast, such as *although* and *whereas*.

Use *although* when the truth is possibly unexpected:

He was still hungry although he had had a large lunch. (You would not expect him to be hungry.)

Although a 30 kg weight was attached, the spring did not break.
(You would expect the spring to break.)

You can put *although* at the start of the sentence or in the middle. If you put it at the start, the two parts of the sentence are separated by a comma.

Use *whereas* when the two facts are opposites:

See-saw A has nothing on the left end, whereas see-saw B has nothing on the right end.

Whereas metal A was attracted to the magnet, metal B was not.

Use a comma to separate the two parts of the sentence.

5   Look at Figure 4.3, and then complete the sentences with *although* or *whereas*.

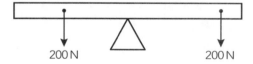

200 N   200 N

Figure 4.3: A see-saw.

a   The force of 200 N on the left of the pivot is closer to the pivot,

.... the force of 200 N on the right is further away from the pivot.

b   .... the forces on each side of the see-saw are equal, the see-saw will turn in a clockwise direction.

c   The forces on each side of the see-saw are equal, ... the moments are different.

d   .... the forces are equal, the see-saw is not balanced, so it is not in equilibrium.

6   Figure 4.4 shows two girls, Sonja and Ria on a see-saw. Use the principle of moments to calculate the distance that Sonja needs to be from the pivot to balance the see-saw.

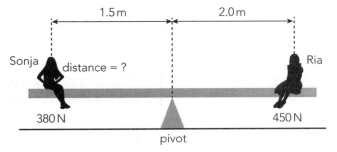

Figure 4.4: Two girls on a see-saw.

Distance: ....

Exercise 4.3 Stability

IN THIS EXERCISE YOU WILL:

Science skills:

*   describe the conditions for the stability of an object.

English skills:

*   use the structure *as....as / not as .... as* to compare the stability of objects

*   practise using *because* to express reason.

KEY WORDS

stable: an object that is unlikely to fall over, often because it has a low centre of gravity and a wide base

centre of gravity: all the mass of an object is considered to be located here

base: lowest part of a structure in contact with a surface

unstable: an object that is likely to fall over, often because it has a high centre of gravity and a narrow base

In this exercise, you will look at how some objects are more **stable** than others and how **centre of gravity** affects stability.

LANGUAGE FOCUS

In Chapter 1, you saw how to form comparatives with adjectives:

You will need a longer plank than that one to lift that box.

Is a pyramid more unstable than a ball?

Another way to compare things is to use *as* [adjective] *as* … or *not so/as* [adjective] *as*…

Use *as* [adjective] *as* when the objects you are comparing are the same or very similar:

The object on the right is as stable as the object on the left.

Use *not so/as* [adjective] *as* when there is a difference between the objects:

The object on the left is not as stable as the object on the right.

LANGUAGE TIP

Likely to (do) is similar in meaning to *probable that it will (do).*

That cup is likely to fall off the table.

You can push them, but they are unlikely to move.

7   Look at Figure 4.5 then complete the sentences using *as* or *not as*.

Figure 4.5: Different objects.

a   The traffic cone and the sports car both have a low centre of gravity so the

traffic cone is .... stable as the sports car.

b   The tall vase has a narrower **base** than the short vase so it is

..........................stable as the short vase.

c   The short vase is ....stable as the traffic cone as they both have wide bases and low centres of gravity.

d   The tall vase is more **unstable** than the lorry, so the lorry is ....
likely to fall over as the vase.

LANGUAGE FOCUS

We use the word *because* to answer the question *why?* Write *because* before the reason, not before the result:

Why did the bookshelf fall down?

The bookshelf fell down <u>because</u> it was unbalanced.

          result   reason

You can also use *because* to introduce an explanation. Start the sentence with *because* then give the reason followed by a comma:

<u>Because</u> *there were many more books at one end than the other, the bookshelf fell down.*

---

8   Look at Figure 4.6 which shows two objects and answer the questions.
Use complete sentences and *because* to give a reason for your answer.

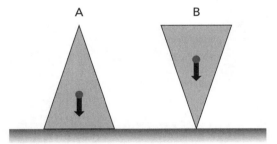

Figure 4.6: Stable and unstable object.

a   Which object is the most stable and why?

....

....

b   Which object is the most unstable and why?

....

....

9   Figure 4.7 shows what happens when a car tilts over. Explain what the pictures show using *as* [adjective] *as* or *not as* [adjective] *as* and the word *because*.

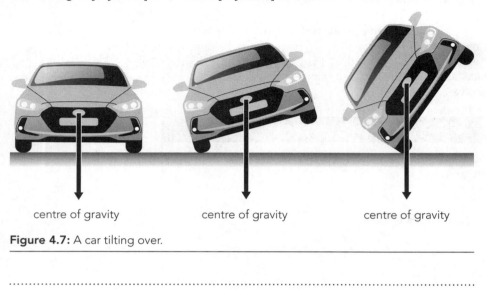

centre of gravity   centre of gravity   centre of gravity

Figure 4.7: A car tilting over.

....

....

....

....

> # Chapter 5
Forces and matter

IN THIS CHAPTER YOU WILL:

Science skills:

- describe the effects of forces on objects and interpret load–extension graphs

- describe pressure and what it depends on.

English skills:

- extend your knowledge of connectives of contrast, including *while* and *whereas*

- use the present continuous.

Exercise 5.1 Forces and springs

IN THIS EXERCISE YOU WILL:

Science skills:

- describe how forces can deform objects

- describe what happens when a force is applied to a spring and interpret load–extension graphs.

English skills:

- meet and practise the key terms related to deformation and forces on springs.

KEY WORDS

deform: changing the size or shape of an object

tensile force: the stretching force acting on an object

extension: the increased length of an object when a load is attached to it

load: the force stretching an object

In this exercise, you will look at how forces can **deform** an object. Objects can be stretched, compressed, bent or twisted by different forces.

1   Fill in the spaces in the paragraph. Use the words below. Not all the words are needed.

compressed   deform   force   permanently   shape   stretched

When you apply a .... to an object, it can .... the

object. When you kick a football, the football becomes .... and

then it will return to its original .... However, if you twist a piece

of silver, it will become .... deformed.

2   If a **tensile force** is applied to a spring, the spring will stretch. Figure 5.1 shows the
apparatus used to investigate how the **extension** of a spring changes when the **load**
on it is increased. Use the blank boxes to renumber the instructions below, so that
the steps to the method are in the correct order.

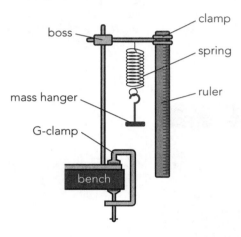

Figure 5.1: Apparatus to investigate the extension of a spring.

Calculate the spring extension by subtracting the original length of the spring (without the mass) from the new length of the spring (with the mass).	☐
Set up the apparatus.	☐
Repeat using different masses.	☐
Record the reading on the ruler where it lines up with the bottom of the mass hanger.	☐
Add a mass to the mass hanger and record the new ruler reading then remove the mass.	☐
Clamp the ruler with zero at the top of the spring.	☐

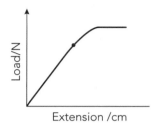

3   Figure 5.2 shows a load–extension graph for a spring.

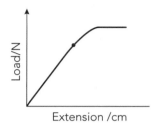

Figure 5.2: Load–extension graph for a spring.

a   What does the straight-line part of the graph show?

....

b   **i**   What is the point called where the graph starts to curve?

....

ii   What will happen if the spring is stretched beyond this point?

....

Exercise 5.2 Pressure

IN THIS EXERCISE YOU WILL:

Science skills:

*   describe pressure and what it depends on.

English skills:

*   review and practise *whereas*, and become familiar with *while* as a connective of contrast.

KEY WORDS

pressure: the force acting per unit area at right angles to a surface

fluid: a liquid or a gas

atmospheric pressure: the pressure felt by an object in the Earth's atmosphere due to particles in the air colliding with it

In this exercise, you will look at **pressure** and what it depends on.

4 Complete the paragraph about pressure using the words below. Not all the words are needed.

> **area**   **density**   **depth**   **force**   **greater**

When a force is applied to an object, the greater the force, the ....

the pressure on the object. Pressure also depends on the ....
that the force is applied to. The pressure on an object in a **fluid** depends on the

.... of the fluid and the .... of the object.

LANGUAGE FOCUS

As you saw in Chapter 4, when you want to contrast two characteristics or facts, you can use the words *but* or *whereas*. However, you can also use the word *while*.

While or *whereas* can do the same job as *but*, but are more appropriate in science. They can go at the beginning or in the middle of the sentence:

While high pressure is associated with clear skies, low pressure is associated with clouds.

High pressure is associated with clear skies, whereas low pressure is associated with rain.

Whereas can only be used when the ideas expressed are opposites:

The weather was good yesterday, whereas the weather today is bad. (good/bad = opposites)

If the ideas are not complete opposites, you can use *while*:

While the weather was good yesterday, today it is better. (good/better = different but not opposites)

---

5 Rewrite each pair of sentences using *while* or *whereas*.

a For a liquid, the pressure at the surface is given by $p = \dfrac{F}{A}$.

The change in pressure due to a column of liquid is given by $\Delta p = \rho g \Delta h$.

....

....

b When we hit a nail with a greater force, the pressure on the nail increases.
The **atmospheric pressure** on the nail remains constant.

....

....

c   If you dive to the bottom of the sea there is a higher pressure acting on you.

     If you climb a mountain there is a lower pressure acting on you.

....

....

6   Read the paragraph below then write two sentences using the information and the word *while*.

> When a force is applied to an object, the pressure on the object depends on the size of the force. When an object is dropped into water, the pressure on the object increases with the depth of the water. Pressure depends on the density of a fluid. Liquids are more dense and exert a higher pressure. Gases are less dense and exert a lower pressure.

....

....

....

....

Exercise 5.3 More about forces and pressure

IN THIS EXERCISE YOU WILL:

Science skills:

- describe forces and pressure.

English skills:

- express things happening at the moment using the present continuous.

In this exercise, you will look at how to use the present continuous tense to describe forces and pressure.

7   Complete the sentences with the *-ing* form of the verbs given in [brackets].

a   The spring is getting longer because Salma is .... [stretch] it.

b   The bike is .... [sink] into the mud, because its narrow tyres have less surface area and exert more pressure on the ground.

c   .... [increase] the load on a spring increases its extension.

LANGUAGE TIP

When you talk about something happening at a particular moment, use the present continuous: *be (am, are, is)* + the *-ing* form of the verb:

The weights <u>are pulling</u> on the springs.

Something <u>is burning</u>!

The ice <u>is making</u> a noise.

d   Pressure in a fluid is .... [act] equally in all directions.

e   Paco is .... [measure] the length of the stretched spring in an experiment.

LANGUAGE FOCUS

When you want to express an intention or aim, for example, when you are explaining why someone is doing something, use *in order to* or *so that*. These phrases can replace *because (we) want to…* or *because (we) need to…*

We use a good-quality metre ruler <u>in order</u> to take accurate measurements.

We use a good-quality metre ruler <u>so that</u> the measurements are accurate.

(We use a good-quality metre rule because we want to take accurate measurements.)

Use *in order to* before a verb. If you cut the sentence after *in order*, it does not look like a complete sentence:

~~We use a good quality metre ruler in order~~
<u>to take accurate measurements</u>.

        ↑
  not a complete sentence

Use *so that* before a subject + verb clause. If you cut the sentence after *so that*, it looks like a complete sentence:

~~We use a good quality metre ruler so that~~
<u>the measurements are accurate</u>.

        ↑
  a complete sentence

---

8   Rewrite the sentences using the phrase in [brackets]. Do not change the meaning of the sentences.

a   Dance hall owners often ask people to remove stiletto heels because they do not want the heels to damage the floor with their high pressure. [so that]

   ....

b   Karen plots a graph of load against extension for a spring because she wants to see whether the extension is directly proportional to the load. [in order to]

   ....

c   Amir does not put too heavy a load on the spring because he does not want the spring to be permanently deformed. [so that]

   ....

d Bungee jumpers use a springy rubber rope because they want to bounce up and down at the bottom of their fall. [in order to]

....

9 Alok lives in a house with a flat roof. The roof is not very strong. Alok's ball has gone on the roof and his uncle is rescuing it. Alok's uncle is crawling along a wooden plank to get the ball so that he does not damage the roof.

Figure 5.3: Rescuing a ball from a flat roof.

Use ideas about force and pressure to explain why Alok's uncle is crawling along a plank to avoid damaging the roof. Some of your verbs should be in the present continuous form. Also include *in order to* and *so that*.

....

....

....

....

> Chapter 6

Energy stores and transfers

IN THIS CHAPTER YOU WILL:

Science skills:

- describe energy stores and energy transfers
- describe energy efficiency and the principle of conservation of energy.

English skills:

- use connectives to talk about the consequences of actions and practise responding to command words
- use comparison words to describe energy efficiency.

Exercise 6.1 Energy stores

IN THIS EXERCISE YOU WILL:

Science skills:

- describe different stores of energy.

English skills:

- review and extend key words about energy stores.

KEY WORDS

energy: quantity that must be changed or transferred to make something happen

In this exercise, you will look at the different ways that **energy** can be stored and some examples of energy stores in everyday life.

1   Find eight words related to energy stores in the word string. Write them on the lines below. One has been done for you.

kineticelasticchemicalinternalthermalnucleargravitationalpotentialstrain

kinetic ....

....

2   Match each energy store with its description.

Energy store	Description
A kinetic energy	**1** energy stored in an object that has changed shape
B gravitational potential energy	**2** the total kinetic and potential energies of the particles in an object
C chemical energy	**3** energy stored in a moving object
D internal energy	**4** energy stored in the nucleus of an atom
E nuclear energy	**5** energy stored in an object when it is lifted up against the force of gravity
F strain energy	**6** energy stored in the bonds between atoms

3   Fill in the spaces to complete the paragraph about the energy stores in a rubber ball. Use the words below.

gravitational potential energy   greater   heated   internal energy

kinetic energy   strain energy

A rubber ball rolling along a surface has .... The faster the ball

rolls, the .... its energy. If you throw the ball into the air, it gains

.... If you squash the ball, it has a store of ....

The ball is made from atoms. If the ball is ...., the atoms vibrate

around more and the ball has more ....

Exercise 6.2 Energy transfers

IN THIS EXERCISE YOU WILL:

Science skills:

- describe energy transfers and how the energy is transferred.

English skills:

- use connectives to talk about the consequences of actions

- practise responding to command words.

KEY WORDS

event: something that happens or takes place, often at a specific time and place

process: a series of actions or steps, often taking place over a long period of time

In this exercise, you will look at how energy is transferred between stores. Energy can be transferred by an **event** or a **process**.

4 Match each way of transferring energy with its description.

Ways of transferring energy	Description
A electrical working	**1** energy transferred by heating
B thermal working	**2** energy transferred by a force
C radiation	**3** energy transferred by an electric current
D mechanical working	**4** energy transferred by a wave

LANGUAGE FOCUS

In physics, you often need to talk about the consequences of actions or observations. These consequences can be a conclusion or a second action:

Observation: *The bulb did not light up when we switched it on.*

Consequence (conclusion): *We knew something was not working.*

Action: *We decided to test the electrical supply and the bulb.*

Consequence (conclusion): *The electricity supply worked, but the bulb did not.*

Consequence (action): *We went to get a new bulb.*

In science, the words *therefore* and *consequently* are often used to connect actions or observations with their consequences. *Therefore* and *consequently* mean the same thing and are used at the start of a sentence followed by a comma. *Therefore* can also be used after *and*.

The bulb did not light up when we switched it on. <u>Therefore</u>, we knew something was not working.

The bulb did not light up when we switched it on, <u>and therefore</u> we knew something was not working.

The electricity supply worked, but the bulb did not. <u>Consequently</u>, we went to get a new bulb.

5   Rewrite the sentences using the words *therefore* or *consequently*. Use the Language focus box to help you.

   a   In an electrical circuit, energy is transferred from the chemical store of the cell to the internal energy of the bulb. The bulb gives out light radiation.

   ....

   ....

   b   Energy from the Sun is transferred by radiation to the Earth. Plants and animals can exist on the Earth.

   ....

   ....

   c   In a car engine, energy is transferred from chemical energy to thermal energy to kinetic energy. The car moves.

   ....

   ....

LANGUAGE TIP

When you want to emphasise the fact that two things share a characteristic or behave in the same way, you can use *both*.

<u>Both</u> light and sound are examples of waves.

6 Rewrite the sentences as one sentence using the word both. Use the Language tip box to help you.

a In an incandescent light bulb, the internal energy of the bulb is transferred by radiation and by heating to the internal energy of the surroundings. It is also transferred to the surroundings by thermal energy transfer.

....

....

b As a ball rolls down a ramp, its gravitational potential energy is transferred to kinetic energy. It is also transferred to the internal energy of the ball.

....

....

LANGUAGE FOCUS

Certain words tell you to write or present your answer to the question in a specific way. You need to know what to do when you see certain command words.
There are several important command words, including *state* and *describe*.

State means 'express in clear terms'.

Describe means 'state the points of a topic/give characteristics and main features'.

---

7 Figure 6.1 shows a diagram of a flashlight. Use it to help you answer the questions.

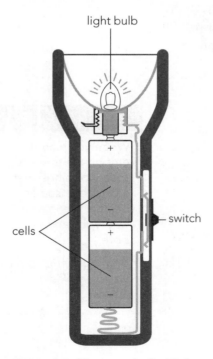

Figure 6.1: Diagram of a flashlight.

a   State how energy is stored in the flashlight when it is switched off.

....

b   Describe the energy transfers that happen when the flashlight is switched on
and how they occur.

....

....

....

....

Exercise 6.3 Energy efficiency

IN THIS EXERCISE YOU WILL:

Science skills:

*   describe energy efficiency and the principle of conservation of energy.

English skills:

*   review and extend words and phrases to compare energy efficiency.

KEY WORDS

efficiency: the fraction (or percentage) of energy supplied that is usefully
transferred

principle of conservation of energy: energy cannot be created or destroyed;
it can only be stored or transferred

In this exercise, you will compare the **efficiency** of different devices and look at the
principle of conservation of energy.

8   Complete the paragraph about energy efficiency. Use the words below.

efficient   heat   useful   wasted

Often, when energy is transferred, some of the energy is transferred to a store

that is not useful. This energy is known as .... energy and it is

usually transferred away as .... A more .... device

transfers a larger percentage of its input energy to .... energy.

LANGUAGE FOCUS

In Chapter 1, you saw how to form comparatives and superlatives from adjectives. In science, you often use *greater*, rather than *bigger* or *larger*:

A *greater* number (of…)

A *greater* impact (on…)

A *greater* (increase)

(These results are) of *greater* interest.

Other key words for comparison are *less* and *the least*. They mean the opposite of *more* and *the most*, and they are used less frequently.

A is *less* (interesting) than B. (B is more interesting than A.)

Out of A, B and C, A is the *least* (interesting). (B and C are more interesting than A.)

You can use *more* and *less* in front of nouns. You will see this again in Chapter 7.

9   The table shows the energy efficiency of some devices.

Device	Efficiency/%
incandescent light bulb	5
petrol engine	30
washing machine motor	70
electric heater	100

Look at the table then fill in the gaps to complete the sentences. Use the words below. Not all the words will be needed.

best   greater   least   less   lower   more   most   worst

a   An incandescent light bulb is the .... efficient device.

b   An electric heater is the .... device in terms of efficiency as it transfers all the chemical energy from a gas power station.

c   A washing machine motor transfers .... energy as useful energy than a petrol engine.

10 Figure 6.2 shows the energy transfers for a ball rolling down a slope.

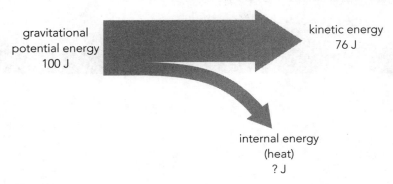

gravitational
potential energy
100 J

kinetic energy
76 J

internal energy
(heat)
? J

Figure 6.2: Energy transfers for a ball rolling down a slope.

a   What does the principle of conservation of energy state about the energy
before and after an energy transfer?

....

b   Use the principle of conservation of energy to calculate the wasted energy.

Wasted energy: ....

Energy resources

Exercise 7.1 Energy resources

KEY WORDS

renewable energy resource: an energy resource that can be replaced when it is used, such as solar power, water waves and biofuels

fossil fuels: natural gas, coal and oil; a non-renewable source of energy

biomass fuel: a renewable energy resource made from plant matter or animal waste; also known as a biofuel

hydroelectric power: using the kinetic energy of water to turn a turbine attached to a generator, which generates electricity

In this exercise, you will look at the different types of energy resources and use comparison words to compare them.

LANGUAGE FOCUS

In Chapter 6, you saw that the following words can be used in front of nouns: *less … than*, *more … than*, *the most*, and *the least*.

Modern houses need <u>less heat than</u> old houses because they have better insulation.

In a block of flats, the flat at the top needs <u>the most energy</u> to heat it. A flat in the middle needs <u>the least energy</u>.

When you compare nouns (things), it is important to know if they refer to things you can count (countable nouns) or that you cannot count (uncountable nouns). Only uncountable nouns work with *less than* and *the least*.

How do you know if a noun is countable? Try a number in front of it or add *-s*.

Resource (countable): You can say *1 resource, 2 resources, 3 resources*.

Plant matter (uncountable): You cannot say *1 plant matter, 2 plant matters, 3 plant matters*.

Material (countable): You can say *material, materials*.

Therefore, you can use plant matter with *less than* and *the least*.

We burn <u>less plant matter than</u> we did centuries ago.

With countable nouns, use *fewer than* and *the fewest*.

Countries further from the Equator generate <u>less solar energy</u>.

Countries further from the Equator build <u>fewer solar farms than</u> wind farms.

You can use *(not) as much/many … as* to express similarity or difference. Use *much* with uncountable nouns and *many* with countable nouns.

Solar power does not produce <u>as much noise pollution as</u> wind power.

You do not need <u>as many wind turbines as</u> solar panels to generate electricity.

1   Look at the words below. Write each one under the correct heading in the table.

electricity   energy   pollutant   pollution   power
solar panel   tree   turbine

Uncountable	Countable

2   Complete the sentences using *less*, *fewer*, *as much* and *as many*.

a   Vehicle manufacturers want to make engines that emit .... pollution.

b   If you use .... electricity, you can help protect the environment.

c   Electric vehicles do not produce .... air pollution as petrol vehicles.

d   **Renewable energy resources** produce .... pollutants than **fossil fuels**.

e   Using renewable energy resources does not cause .... damage to the Earth as using fossil fuels.

f   Do you think that in the future people will buy .... cars that run on renewable energy as cars that run on fossil fuels?

g   The United States produces the most crude oil. Most countries produce

.... barrels of crude oil than the United States.

3   Jeanne is studying energy in her country. She has made a pie chart and written notes. Complete the sentences below using information from her pie chart and her notes.

Energy resources

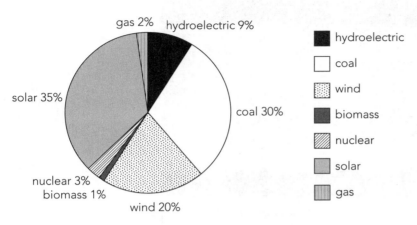

Figure 7.1: Energy resources pie chart.

Energy producer	Number of
Nuclear power station	30
Gas power station	28
Wind farm	2000
Solar farm	3900

LANGUAGE TIP

You can use phrases like *twice/three times as much/ many* + noun + *as* to compare quantities. *Almost nine times* <u>*as many people*</u> *live in the USA* <u>*as*</u> *live in Canada.*

a   This country does not use as much **biomass fuel** ....as gas...............

b   **Hydroelectric power** is used three ....

c   There are fewer ....

d   This country uses nearly ten times ....

e   This country has almost twice as .... farms.

f   This country uses almost ....

Exercise 7.2 Comparing energy resources

IN THIS EXERCISE YOU WILL:

Science skills:

- compare different energy resources.

English skills:

- practise key vocabulary and review some ways of comparing and contrasting.

KEY WORDS

nuclear fuel: a material, such as uranium or plutonium, that is a store of nuclear energy

In this exercise, you will compare energy resources and think about which energy resource is most suitable for a particular region.

4 Match each energy resource to how it is used to produce energy.

Energy resource	Description
1 biofuel	**A** energy is produced by the kinetic energy of moving air
2 nuclear fuel	**B** energy is produced by burning coal, oil or natural gas
3 hydroelectric	**C** energy is produced by burning plant matter or animal waste
4 fossil fuels	**D** energy is produced by radioactive decay
5 wind power	**E** energy is produced by the kinetic energy of moving water

5 a   Write at least three sentences comparing the following energy resources:
renewable energy resources, fossil fuels and nuclear fuels.

Use the phrases below and your own ideas.

as much as   less than   more than   the least   the most

....

....

....

....

....

....

b   Choose the resource you think is most suitable for your region. Give reasons
for your choice.

For example: *The most suitable resource for my region is the renewable energy
resource wind. This is because we have more hours of wind than sun. Wind is
safer than nuclear fuels and produces less pollution than fossil fuels.*

....

....

....

....

Exercise 7.3 Generating electricity

IN THIS EXERCISE YOU WILL:

Science skills:

*   compare the generation of electricity using different energy resources.

English skills:

*   practise responding to the command words *compare* and *explain*.

KEY WORDS

power station: an industrial facility where electricity is generated from fossil
fuels, nuclear fuels and renewable energy resources

In this exercise, you will look at how electricity is generated from different energy resources and compare their impact on the environment.

6 The diagram shows how a fossil fuel **power station** generates electricity. Look at the diagram, and then complete the steps using the words below.

coal   generator coil   heat   high pressure steam   turbine

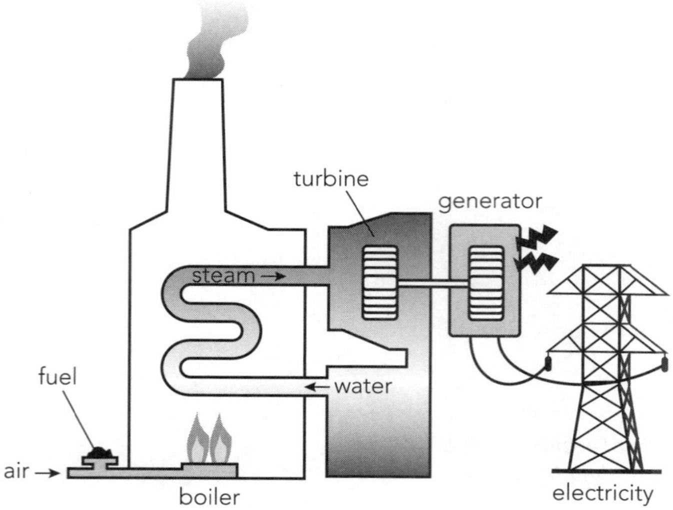

Figure 7.2: A fossil fuel power station.

Step 1: .... is burned in the boiler to produce thermal energy.

Step 2: This energy is used to .... the water.

Step 3: This generates ....

Step 4: This turns the blades of the ....

Step 5: As the blades move, they turn the .... and electricity is produced.

LANGUAGE FOCUS

As you saw in Chapter 6, it is important to understand command words so that you know what you are expected to do. Understanding command words will also help you decide what words you should use in your answer.

Compare: This means to identify or comment on similarities and / or differences. You may also see *compare and contrast*. Words and phrases like *as … as*, *not as … as*, *less … than*, and comparative adjectives are useful for this.

Explain: This means to set out purposes or reasons / make the relationships between things evident / provide why and / or how and support with relevant evidence (e.g. *cause and effect, action and consequence*). Words like *first, then, next, because* and *consequently* help here.

LANGUAGE TIP

A good expression meaning 'talking about' or 'with reference to' is *in terms of*.

Wind power is better than fossil fuels in terms of carbon dioxide emitted.

7 Electricity can be produced from nuclear fuel in a nuclear power station and coal in a fossil fuel power station.

Write two sentences for each of the following. Use the Language focus box to help you.

a Explain how using nuclear fuel and coal in power stations can damage the environment.

....

....

....

....

b Compare nuclear fuel and coal in terms of their energy efficiency.

....

....

....

....

> Chapter 8
Work and power

Exercise 8.1 Work done

KEY WORDS

work done: the amount of energy transferred when a force moves an object through a distance in the direction of the force

LANGUAGE TIP

Many terms in science consist of two words working together to name one concept. Notice that with this kind of term, the 'thing' is the second word, and the first word describes it:

static electricity
magnetic force
clamp stand
wind turbine

In this exercise, you will look at **work done**. If you exert a force on an object and the object moves in the direction of the force then you have done work on the object. If you exert a force on the object and the object does not move in the direction of the force then you have not done work.

1   a   i   Find seven words related to work done in the word string. Write them on the lines below. One has been done for you.

transferdirectionjoulesenergykineticdistanceforce

kinetic
....

....

    ii   Which word in part **i** is a store of energy? Write the word.

        ....

b   Complete these sentences using the words in part **ai**. You will use some words twice.

    i   Work is defined as the product of .... and

        ....

    ii   The unit of work done is ....

    iii   No work is done when we apply a .... but the object does

        not move in the direction of the ....

    iv   The greater the .... moved in the .... of the force, the greater the work done.

    v   Work done is equal to the amount of .... transferred.

2 **a**   Reorder the letters to make words or terms. Match four of the words to their definitions.

        ctikine   **nryeeg**   **okwr oedn**   **oljues**   **ntialtepo**

Word	Definition
....	transferred to an object when work is done on the object
....	the energy stored by a moving object
....	the unit of energy
....	the energy stored by an object due to its position relative to another object

  b   Write your own short definition of the fifth term.

        ....

        ....

Exercise 8.2 Power

IN THIS EXERCISE YOU WILL:

Science skills:

- describe the relationship between power, work done and time taken.

English skills:

- use the connective *as* to express two actions happening at the same time.

KEY WORDS

power: the rate at which energy is transferred or work is done

watt: the unit of power; one watt is equal to one joule of energy transferred per second

In this exercise, you will look at **power**, which is the amount of energy transferred per second or the rate of doing work. The unit of power is the **watt**. For example, person A and person B climb the same number of stairs. Person B climbs the stairs in a shorter time than person A. Person B is said to have greater power than person A.

LANGUAGE FOCUS

When you discuss work and power, and in particular energy transfers, you often talk about two things that happen at the same time that are related to each other. For example:

Force is applied to the object. The object moves.

To make it clear that the two actions happen at the same time, use the word *as* before the action that starts the energy transfer.

<u>As</u> you apply a force to the object, the object moves.

The object moves <u>as</u> you apply a force to it.

Notice that when you start the sentence with *as*, you need a comma between the two actions.

Remember that it is important to be accurate in science, which means it is important to use words like *as*, or *first* and *then*.

*You position your feet correctly. You apply a force to the object.
The object moves.*

Does the object move when you apply force to it, or does it move later?

*<u>First,</u> you position your feet correctly. <u>Then</u> you apply a force to the object.
<u>As</u> you apply the force to the object, it moves.*

3 **a** Read the text and underline the sentences that use *as*.

When a person exerts a force on an object they are doing work. The time taken to do the work decreases as the power of the person increases. As the amount of energy transferred increases, power also increases. Coal power stations produce pollutants as they generate electricity. The ratio of the useful power output to the power input is called the efficiency of the power station.

b Complete the table with the information in the sentences you underlined in part **a**. The first one has been done for you.

Action that starts the energy transfer	Action that happens at the same time
the power of the person increases	the time taken to do the work decreases

4 **a** Read the following sentences and decide if they are True or False. Circle your answer.

   i Salima runs 100 m in 32 seconds. Her speed increases as she runs the next 100 m because her power has decreased. (True / False)

   ii Anny is lifting a 10 kg weight. As she lifts it for the second time, she takes less time to make the lift so her power has increased. (True / False)

   iii Sofia climbs a mountain. As she climbs the last part, she climbs more slowly, so there is an increase in her power. (True / False)

   iv Arkin is pushing a trolley. He pushes it 2 m in a certain time. The time it takes to push the trolley the next 2 m decreases as his power decreases. (True / False)

   b Now rewrite the false sentences and correct the information.

   ....

   ....

   ....

   ....

   ....

   ....

Exercise 8.3 Work and power

IN THIS EXERCISE YOU WILL:

Science skills:

- describe work and power in real life.

English skills:

- use *it is* + adjective + *to* + verb to describe actions.

KEY WORDS

gravitational potential energy: the energy that an object has when it is raised up against the gravitational force

In this exercise, you will look at examples of work and power in real life and use adjectives to describe them.

LANGUAGE FOCUS

When you want to describe an action as difficult, easy, important, etc. then use this pattern:

It is (easy/difficult/important/helpful/challenging) to + verb

or

It is not (easy/difficult/important/helpful/challenging) to + verb

For example:

In long distance running, <u>it is important to conserve</u> energy for the whole race. <u>It is not sensible to use</u> all your energy at the start of the race.

If you want to add a person, add *for* + (person) after the adjective.

It is easy <u>for a fit runner</u> to complete the race.

It is useful <u>for athletes</u> to estimate the required energy in order to eat the right food.

5   Read the following paragraph, and then complete the question.

Work is done when a force exerted on an object moves the object in the same direction as the force. For example, when you lift a football up, the football gains **gravitational potential energy**. Work is done in lifting the football because the direction of movement is in the same direction as the force. It is possible to exert a force on an object without moving the object. In this case, no work has been done by the force.
Another example of a force doing no work is when a force is applied and the movement of the object is not in the direction of the force.

Look around you and find four different examples of work done and power. Then complete the table. One example has been done for you.

Example	Explanation in terms of work done or power
kicking a football	When you kick a football, you are doing work on the football.

6   Use the words below to describe the action in each picture. Words can be used more than once. The first one has been done for you.

difficult   easy   fast   heavy   helpful   high   important   slow   useful

Picture	Description
	The weights are not very heavy so it is easy for the person to lift them. As the weights get higher, they gain gravitational potential energy.

LANGUAGE TIP

A good scientific verb meaning 'get more' is *gain*. You can *gain weight/ height*, etc.

7 Write a sentence about each of these pairs of actions. Use *easier to* + verb and the word *because*. Also refer to power or work done.

Example:

Miranda leads a friendly horse.

Jasmina leads a horse that does not want to move.

It is easier for Miranda to lead her horse than Jasmina because Jasmina's horse does not want to move. Jasmina needs more power to lead her horse.

a Pushing a lighter box

Pushing a heavier box

....

....

b Walking up the stairs

Running up the stairs

....

....

c Dyan lifts a 50 N weight.

Peter lifts a 100 N weight the same distance.

....

....

Chapter 9

The kinetic particle model of matter

Exercise 9.1 Changes of state

KEY WORDS

states of matter: solid, liquid or gas

changes of state: changing from one state of matter to another

In this exercise, you will review your knowledge about the three **states of matter** and look at **changes of state**.

1   Complete the table about the three states of matter.

State of matter	Shape	Volume	Property
	rigid and fixed shape	fixed volume	cannot be squashed
	no rigid or fixed shape and takes the shape of its container	fixed volume	cannot be squashed
	no rigid or fixed shape and expands to fill its container	no fixed volume	can be squashed

2   Figure 9.1 shows the changes of state for water. Label the diagram using the words below.

condensing   evaporation   freezing   melting

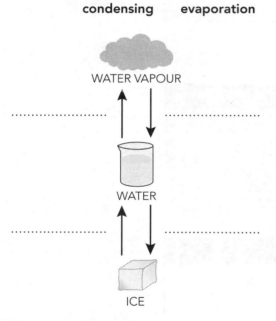

Figure 9.1: Changes of state for water.

LANGUAGE FOCUS

In science, it is important to use verbs in the correct form. When you write about facts, you need to use the present simple:

A gas <u>expands</u> to fit its container.

Gas particles <u>move</u> randomly.

A gas is singular, and the verb ends with *s*: *expands*

Particles is plural, and the verb does not end with *s*: *move*

When the verb is a negative:

A liquid <u>does not</u> expand to fit its container.

The particles in a solid <u>do not</u> move randomly.

A liquid is singular and *does not* is in front of a verb. The verb has no *s* at the end.

Particles is plural and *do not* is in front of the verb. The verb has no *s* at the end.

The verbs *be* and *can* work differently from other verbs:

be	it/he/she is/is not	we/you/they are/are not
can	can + verb	cannot + verb

Check your work after you finish and look carefully at your verbs. Check that:

* singular subjects have the correct verb form
* plural subjects have the correct verb form.

Remember: if the subject is plural, you do not need an *s* at the end of the verb.

3 a Circle the correct verb form in each sentence.

 i   When a gas *condense / condenses*, it changes into a liquid.

 ii Solids *melt / melts* and become liquids when they are heated.

 iii When a liquid *evaporate / evaporates*, it changes into a gas.

 iv Gases do not *solidify / solidifies* into liquids.

 b Describe what happens to the shape and volume of a gas when it is cooled. Use the present simple.

 ....

 ....

 ....

 ....

LANGUAGE TIP

Use *when* + present simple to describe things that are always true.

When water is heated to 100 °C, it evaporates.

Exercise 9.2 Kinetic particle model of matter

IN THIS EXERCISE YOU WILL:

Science skills:

- use the kinetic particle model of matter to explain the arrangement and motion of particles.

English skills:

- become familiar with formal verbs used in science.

KEY WORDS

kinetic particle model of matter: a model in which matter consists of moving particles

In this exercise, you will look at the **kinetic particle model of matter**, which is used by scientists to explain the arrangement and motion of particles in solids, liquids and gases.

4   Match each state of matter with the arrangement and movement of its particles.

State of matter	Arrangement and movement of particles
A solid	**1** widely separated; move freely about
B liquid	**2** close together in a regular pattern; vibrate about a fixed position
C gas	**3** less close together and arranged randomly; vibrate and move about

5   Complete the sentences about the motion of particles and temperature. Use the words below.

absolute zero   faster   gain   lose   no   slower

a   When a substance is heated, its particles .... kinetic energy.

The particles move ....

b   If the substance is cooled, its particles .... kinetic energy and

the particles move ....

c   .... is the lowest possible temperature that a substance can

reach. At this point, the particles have .... kinetic energy and
they stop moving.

LANGUAGE FOCUS

Science often uses formal verbs, rather than the informal verbs used in normal conversation, because scientific language needs to be precise. With precise language, everyone understands the same thing. This means that verbs that consist of two words in normal conversation are frequently replaced in scientific discussion by verbs that consist of one word. The verb *get* is not generally used at all.

The temperature goes up.

The temperature <u>increases</u>. The temperature <u>rises</u>.

When you blow into a balloon, it gets bigger.

When you <u>inflate</u> a balloon, it <u>expands</u>.

What happens when iron gets hot?

What <u>happens</u> when iron <u>is heated</u>?

Sometimes a scientific verb consists of two words, but is more formal than the usual verb.

When one particle bumps into another, energy goes from the first particle to the second particle.

When one particle <u>collides with</u> another particle, energy is <u>transferred</u>.

---

6   **a**   Rewrite the sentences to use formal verbs. Use the Language focus box to
help you.

   i   When a liquid is heated, the particles get more kinetic energy.

   ....

   ii   The particles of a solid start to vibrate more as the temperature of the
solid goes up.

   ....

   iii   When a gas is made hotter, the particles of the gas bump into each other
and the walls of the container more frequently.

   ....

b   Explain what happens to the arrangement and motion of the particles in a substance as it changes state from solid to gas. Use formal verbs in your explanation.

....

....

....

....

....

....

Exercise 9.3 Brownian motion and behaviour of gases

IN THIS EXERCISE YOU WILL:

Science skills:

- describe Brownian motion as evidence for the kinetic particle model of matter

- use the kinetic model of matter to explain the behaviour of solids, liquids and gases.

English skills:

- recognise and use the correct forms of verbs

- make predictions using the modal verb *will*.

KEY WORDS

Brownian motion: the motion of small particles suspended in a liquid or gas, caused by molecular bombardment

In this exercise, you will look at how **Brownian motion** is evidence for the kinetic particle model of matter and how the kinetic model can explain the behaviour of solids, liquids and gases.

7 Figure 9.2 shows a smoke cell.

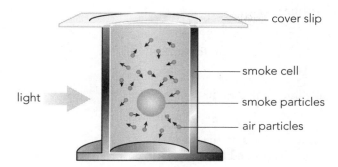

cover slip

smoke cell

light

smoke particles

air particles

Figure 9.2: A smoke cell.

a Read the paragraph and <u>underline</u> the verbs.

> A smoke cell can be used to demonstrates Brownian motion. The smoke
>
> cell contain air particles and smoke particles. The smoke particles moves
>
> in a random motion and changes direction frequently. This happens
>
> because fast-moving air particles collides with the smoke particles.

b Five of the verbs are not in the correct form. Write the correct verbs above the incorrect verbs.

LANGUAGE FOCUS

To make a prediction about something that you are sure is going to happen, use the modal verb *will / will not* + verb.

Lakes <u>will evaporate</u> because of climate change.

There <u>will not</u> be enough water in the lakes for the animals that live near them.

Notice the difference between a prediction and a fact.

Lakes will evaporate because of climate change. (This is something that you feel sure will happen.)

Water evaporates faster as the temperature increases. (This a scientific fact.)

8 Fill in the gaps to predict what will happen.

    a If a bottle of perfume is opened, the particles of perfume .... into the air.

    b If hydrogen gas is put into a larger container, it .... to fit the new container.

    c Sugar particles .... more quickly in a hot drink than in a cold drink.

9 Use the kinetic model of matter to explain why the pressure of a gas on the walls of its container increases when the gas is heated. Use formal verbs and the correct forms.

....

....

....

....

....

....

> Chapter 10
Thermal properties of matter

Exercise 10.1 Thermal expansion

KEY WORDS

thermal expansion: the increase in volume of a material when its temperature rises

Most materials expand when they are heated. In this exercise, you will look at the **thermal expansion** of solids, liquids and gases at a constant pressure.

1   Complete the sentences about thermal expansion. Use the words below. Not all of the words are needed.

contracts   faster   kinetic   least   less   more

most   slower

When a substance is heated, the particles of the substance gain ....

energy. They move .... and push each other apart.

The substance expands. When a substance is cooled, it ....

Gases expand the .... when they are heated. Liquids generally

expand .... than gases, and solids expand the ....

LANGUAGE FOCUS

In physics, you often need to describe your observations (what you see, smell, hear or feel), then draw conclusions and explain them. Imagine that you have two beakers of water, one hot and one cold, and two metal spoons.
You put one spoon in the cold water and one spoon in the hot water.

Observations (what you can see, feel, etc.):

The spoon remains cold when it is placed in the cold water.
(You touch the spoon, you feel the cold.)

The spoon becomes hot when it is placed in the hot water.
(You touch the spoon, you feel the heat.)

Conclusion (what you know has happened):

Heat is transferred from the water to the spoon. (You cannot see the heat transferring, but you know it has happened.)

Explanation for the conclusion (why you think it has happened):

Metal conducts heat / is a good conductor of heat. (You cannot see or feel this, but it is a logical conclusion.)

Observations, conclusions and explanations use the present simple verb form.

Active (subject + verb): *The spoon remains cold …*

Passive: *Heat is transferred …*

Note that *when + is / are* is often used:

… when it is placed in the cold water.

2   Figure 10.1 shows the thermal expansion of a steel rod. Read each statement
and tick (✓) whether it is an observation, a conclusion or an explanation for
the conclusion.

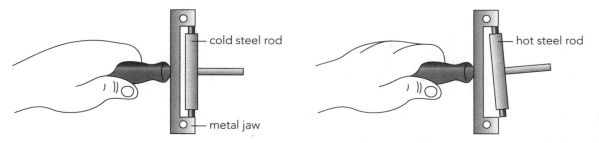

Figure 10.1: Thermal expansion of a steel rod.

Statement	Observation	Conclusion	Explanation
Metals expand when they are heated because the particles gain energy and move faster and take up more space / move further apart.			
The cold steel rod fits inside the gap in the metal jaw.			
When steel is heated, it expands.			
The hot steel rod is too long to fit inside the gap in the metal jaw.			

LANGUAGE TIP

The verb most frequently used with *conclusion* is *draw*; you *draw a conclusion*. In this context, *draw* is not related to lines or pencils but is from an old meaning: 'to extract or pull' (e.g. *draw teeth*, *draw curtains*).

3   Figure 10.2 shows a tyre in summer and winter. Write your observations about
the tyre in summer and winter, write a conclusion and give an explanation for the
conclusion. Use the Language focus box to help you.

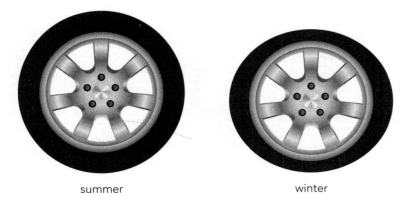

summer   winter

Figure 10.2: A tyre in summer and winter.

Observations:

....

....

Conclusion:

....

....

Explanation for the conclusion:

....

....

Exercise 10.2 Uses of thermal expansion

IN THIS EXERCISE YOU WILL:

Science skills:

• describe some uses of thermal expansion.

English skills:

• practise expressing conclusions and deductions.

KEY WORDS

bimetallic strip: two different metals joined together

In this exercise, you will look at some uses of thermal expansion, such as a thermometer and a fire alarm bell.

4 Figure 10.3 shows an outdoor thermometer. Fill in the gaps to explain how the thermometer works. Use the words below. Not all the words need to be used.

Figure 10.3: An outdoor thermometer.

contracts   decreases   expands   increases   temperature

As the .... of the air increases, the temperature of the liquid in the

thermometer .... The liquid .... and the level of

the liquid in the tube rises.

5 Figure 10.4 shows an electric fire alarm bell. It contains a **bimetallic strip**.
   During a fire, the air around the fire alarm gets hot.

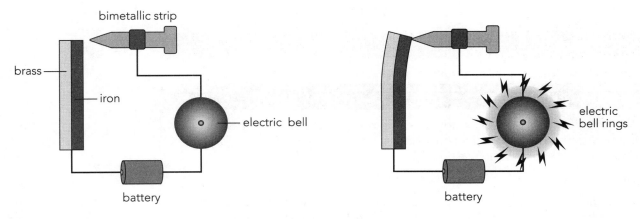

Figure 10.4: An electric fire alarm bell.

a Describe how the electric fire alarm bell works.

....

....

....

LANGUAGE FOCUS

It is useful to know which expressions to use to introduce your conclusion. Good expressions are:

Therefore, we can conclude that …

It can be concluded that …

(This is) due to (the fact that) …

(This is) because of …

The expression can be followed by a clause (like a complete sentence):

<u>*Therefore, we can conclude that*</u> *copper expands when it is heated.*

<u>*It can be concluded that*</u> *copper expands when it is heated.*

<u>*This is due to the fact that*</u> *copper expands when it is heated.*

(This is) due to … and (this is) because of … can be followed by a noun phrase (with a noun, a pronoun or an -ing form, but no verb):

<u>*This is due to*</u> *copper expanding when heated.*

<u>*This is because of*</u> *copper expanding when heated.*

b Give two conclusions that you can draw about the metals in the bimetallic strip. Use the expressions in the Language focus box above.

....

....

....

....

LANGUAGE FOCUS

As a scientist, you need to be able to express a deduction. A deduction is an educated guess based on considering the known facts. To express a deduction, scientists often use:

Therefore / Because / As and … must + verb

The iron in a bimetallic strip bends more than the brass when the bimetallic strip is heated. <u>*Therefore,*</u> *the brass* <u>*must expand*</u> *more than the iron.*

<u>*Because*</u> *the iron in a bimetallic strip bends more than the brass, when the bimetallic strip is heated, the brass* <u>*must expand*</u> *more than the iron.*

6   Write a deduction about each of the following observations. Use *therefore*, *because* or *as* and *must* + verb.

   a   A wooden door is difficult to close in summer.

   ....

   b   When a mercury thermometer is put into a beaker of ice, the level of the mercury drops.

   ....

   c   Gases expand as they heat up.

   ....

Exercise 10.3 Energy, temperature and changes of state

IN THIS EXERCISE YOU WILL:

Science skills:

- relate energy supplied to increase in temperature
- describe what happens to the temperature during changes of state.

English skills:

- practise using key vocabulary for changes of state.

KEY WORDS

evaporation: changing from a liquid to a gas at any temperature

In this exercise, you are going to look at how the internal energy of an object changes when its temperature is increased and what happens to the temperature when a substance changes state.

7   Are these sentences about energy and temperature true or false? Circle the correct answers.

   a   Internal energy is the total kinetic energy of all the particles in an object. *True / False*

   b   When thermal energy is supplied to an object, its temperature increases. *True / False*

   c   Increasing the temperature of an object, increases the kinetic energy of its particles and they move faster. *True / False*

d A cup of 65°C coffee has a higher temperature than a 22°C swimming pool, so it stores more internal energy. *True / False*

8 Figure 10.5 shows a graph of temperature against time for ice being heated.

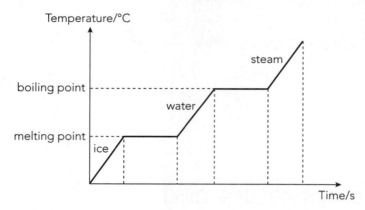

Figure 10.5: A graph of temperature against time for ice being heated.

a **i** Give the melting point of water at standard atmospheric pressure.

....

ii Give the boiling point of water at standard atmospheric pressure.

....

b Describe what happens to the temperature as the ice is heated and becomes steam.

....

....

....

....

c Energy is being supplied to the ice to heat it. Explain why the temperature stays the same when the ice is melting.

....

9   Figure 10.6 shows puddles of water on a sunny day.

Figure 10.6: Puddles of water on a sunny day.

a   Use the kinetic particle model of matter to describe the **evaporation** of the
water in the puddles.

....

....

....

....

b   Use the kinetic particle model of matter to explain why evaporation
causes cooling.

....

....

....

....

Thermal energy transfers

Exercise 11.1 Conduction

KEY WORDS

thermal conductor: a substance that conducts thermal energy

thermal insulator: a substance that conducts very little thermal energy

In this exercise, you are going to look at how materials can either be **thermal conductors** or **thermal insulators**.

1   Are these sentences true or false? (Circle) the correct answer.

    a   Conduction occurs mainly in solids. *True / False*

    b   Thermal energy transfers from a cooler area to a hotter area. *True / False*

    c   Conduction is the transfer of thermal energy by vibrating particles. *True / False*

    d   Metal is a better thermal insulator than wood. *True / False*

LANGUAGE FOCUS

When you write about facts and processes in physics, use the present simple. However, when the scientist or thing carrying out an action is not important or is unknown, use the passive. In a passive sentence, the action is more important than who or what is carrying out the action.

They heat water using a Bunsen burner. (present simple active)

Water is heated using a Bunsen burner. (present simple passive)

The object of the active sentence becomes the subject of the passive sentence:

Water …

Decide if the new subject is singular or plural and add *is, are,* (or *is not* or *are not*):

Water is …

Add the past participle of the verb:

Water is heated …

Complete the sentence with any other information:

Water is heated using a Bunsen burner.

The past participle of regular verbs is made using the verb + *-ed*:

heat – heated

The past participle of irregular verbs is the third 'column' when you look at a verb table:

make – made – made

put – put – put

2   Rewrite the sentences using the present simple passive.

For example:

A frying pan conducts thermal energy to cook the eggs.

Thermal energy is conducted by a frying pan to cook the eggs.

a   When you touch a hot pan, the thermal energy transfers to your body by conduction.

Thermal energy ....

b   The metal spoon takes in heat from the hot soup by conduction.

Heat ....

c   When you put a slice of cheese on a hot burger, the cheese melts because thermal energy transfers from the burger to the cheese.

The slice of cheese ....

3   Figure 11.1 shows the apparatus used in an experiment to investigate which metal rod is the best thermal conductor. Describe the experiment, using the present simple passive. Use the verbs below to help you.

LANGUAGE TIP

In science, equipment is usually referred to as *apparatus*.

heat   melt   transfer

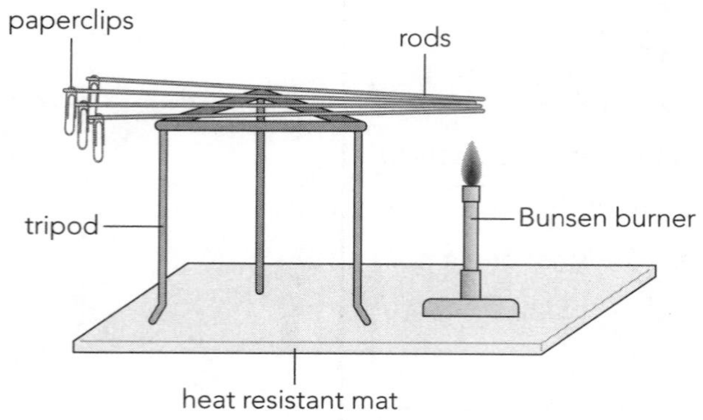

Figure 11.1: Experiment to investigate thermal conduction.

....

....

....

....

....

....

Exercise 11.2 Convection

IN THIS EXERCISE YOU WILL:

Science skills:

- describe convection and convection currents.

English skills:

- practise describing diagrams.

KEY WORDS

convection: the transfer of thermal energy through a material by the movement of the material itself

convection current: the transfer of thermal energy by the motion of a fluid

In this exercise, you will look at how thermal energy is transferred by **convection** in liquids and gases and what a **convection current** is.

4   The table shows examples of thermal energy transfers. Tick (✓) whether each example is conduction or convection.

Thermal energy transfer	Conduction	Convection
An electric heater heating a whole room		
Ice melting in your hand		
Using a hair dryer to dry your hair		
A metal spoon gets hot when left in a cup of hot tea		

5   Figure 11.2 shows convection currents in a pan of water on a gas cooker. Fill in the gaps to explain how a convection current is formed. Use the words below. Not all of the words are needed.

contracts   decreases   downwards   expands   increases

less   more   upwards

Figure 11.2: Convection currents in a pan of water.

Thermal energy is transferred from the gas to the water in the pan.

The water at the bottom of the pan is heated and .... Its density

.... and it flows .... The water at the top of the

pan is colder and .... dense. It flows .... to replace the warmer water.

LANGUAGE FOCUS

Diagrams are useful because they can summarise information and ideas in a visual way. They often show how apparatus is positioned, and arrows indicating direction are frequently used. Here are some useful words and phrases to help you to describe diagrams.

General:

This diagram shows …

The arrow(s) indicate(s) …

(X) is connected to (Y) by a (piece of apparatus) …

Position:

on the right   on the left   the left-hand/right-hand (diagram)

in the centre   below   above   between

at the left-hand/right-hand end (of the rod)   at the top/bottom (of the spring)

(X) is surrounded by …

Movement:

flow   pass   travel   transfer   leave   circulate   pivot   rotate drop   rise

towards   away from   to   from   along   across   through around   throughout   up   down

6   Figure 11.3 shows how a sea breeze is formed by a convection current during the day. Describe what is shown by the diagram. Use the Language focus box to help you.

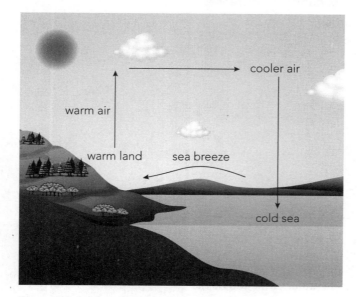

Figure 11.3: How a sea breeze is formed.

....

....

....

....

....

....

Exercise 11.3 Thermal energy radiation and reducing energy transfers

KEY WORDS

infrared radiation: electromagnetic radiation with a wavelength greater than that of visible light; sometimes known as thermal energy radiation

vacuum: a space with no particles in it

In this exercise, you are going to look at energy transfers by **infrared radiation** and how to reduce unwanted thermal energy transfers.

LANGUAGE FOCUS

When you use an adjective (*hot, cold, shallow, long*, etc.) with a noun, the adjective goes before the noun:

a *hot* piece of metal   *cold* water   a *shallow* dish   a *long* spring

Most materials can function as nouns and adjectives. When they act as adjectives, they go before the noun:

a *glass* rod   a *metal* spoon   a *plastic* container   *iron* filings
a *paper* filter

Compound nouns are made by putting two nouns together:

Bunsen burner   *clamp stand*   *physics experiment*   *metre rule*

In a compound noun, the second word is the 'thing' and the first word is like an adjective describing the thing. Notice that there are compound nouns that have merged to form one word over time:

classroom   *notebook*   *toothbrush*   *football*

Sometimes, the two words can be written in two ways:

milk chocolate   *chocolate milk*

In order to work out the meaning, remember that the second word indicates the thing:

Milk chocolate is for eating.

Chocolate milk is for drinking.

7   a   (Circle) the correct compound noun in each pair.

        i   ultraviolet radiation / radiation ultraviolet

        ii   light visible / visible light

        iii   clamp stand / stand clamp

        iv   bulblight / lightbulb

        v   convection heater / heater convection

    b   What is the difference between:

        i   Firewood and a wood fire?

          ....

          ....

        ii   Candle wax and a wax candle?

          ....

          ....

8   **a**   Are the following statements about infrared radiation true or false?
Write T or F next to each statement.

    i   All objects emit infrared radiation. ....

    ii   Cold objects emit more infrared radiation than hot objects.

    ....

    iii   Infrared radiation is an electromagnetic wave. ....

    iv   Infrared radiation cannot travel through a **vacuum**. ....

  b   Figure 11.4 shows a matt black plate next to a shiny white plate.

Figure 11.4: A matt black plate next to a shiny white plate.

    i   Which plate is the best absorber of infrared radiation?

    ....

    ii   Which plate is the best reflector of infrared radiation?

    ....

    iii   Which plate is the best emitter of infrared radiation?

    ....

9   Thermal energy transfers can be useful or not useful. Figure 11.5 shows a vacuum
flask. A vacuum flask is designed to reduce unwanted energy transfers.

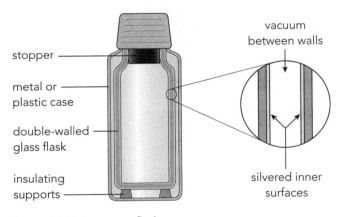

Figure 11.5: A vacuum flask.

> **LANGUAGE TIP**
>
> To give the main use of something, use *to* + verb:
>
> *You can use a clamp to hold things.*
>
> *A thermometer can be used to check the increase in temperature.*

a   Hot liquid is put into the vacuum flask but the stopper is not put in.
    Describe how the thermal energy from the hot liquid is transferred to
    the surroundings.

    ....

    ....

    ....

b   Describe how the structure of a vacuum flask reduces thermal energy loss
    by conduction.

    ....

    ....

    ....

c   Describe how the silvered surfaces inside the walls of the glass flask keep the
    liquid hot.

    ....

    ....

⟩ Chapter 12
Sound

IN THIS CHAPTER YOU WILL:

Science skills:

- describe how sounds are produced and the properties of sound
- describe the range of human hearing and how to measure the speed of sound.

English skills:

- practise using the first conditional *will*
- practise answering questions beginning with *how*.

Exercise 12.1 Producing sounds

IN THIS EXERCISE YOU WILL:

Science skills:

- describe how sounds are produced and transmitted.

English skills:

- use key terms related to production of sounds.

KEY WORDS

transmit (sound): sound energy is transferred from one place to another

In this exercise, you will look at how sounds are produced and how musical instruments can produce sounds in different ways.

1   Sounds can be produced by vibrations in musical instruments.
    Match the word halves to make seven instruments.

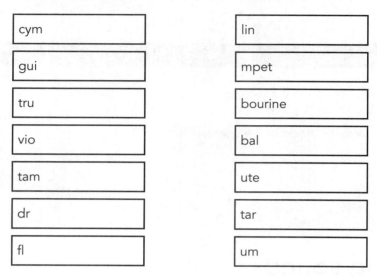

cym	lin
gui	mpet
tru	bourine
vio	bal
tam	ute
dr	tar
fl	um

2   Fill in the gaps to complete the sentences about how sounds are produced and
    transmitted. Use the words below. Words can be used more than once.

    air   eardrums   ears   particles   source

    a   Sounds are caused by a .... vibrating. This causes the

        .... in the air to vibrate.

    b   These cause other .... to vibrate and the vibrations are passed

        through the ....

    c   We can hear sounds because the vibrations reach our ....

        where they cause our .... to vibrate.

3   Figure 12.1 shows three musical instruments. Explain how sound is produced by
    each of the instruments.

Figure 12.1: Drum, guitar and flute.

Drum:...

Guitar:...

Flute:..

Exercise 12.2 Properties of sounds

KEY WORDS

longitudinal wave: a wave in which the particles vibrate backwards and forwards, along the direction of travel of the wave

amplitude: the greatest height or depth of a wave from its undisturbed position

frequency: the number of complete vibrations or waves per unit time

cathode ray oscilloscope: an instrument that shows a sound wave as a trace (line) on a screen

In this exercise, you will learn how to describe the properties of sounds. Sounds are **longitudinal waves**.

4   Find six words in the word search that are useful for describing sounds.

F	A	M	P	L	I	T	U	D	E
K	T	X	C	B	P	C	L	Z	F
G	O	T	F	S	Q	O	I	L	R
I	O	N	X	U	P	K	S	O	E
U	H	P	G	F	J	E	L	U	Q
L	E	I	A	W	D	B	E	D	U
L	R	T	F	V	O	V	U	D	E
W	T	C	E	E	M	G	U	V	N
K	Z	H	D	H	N	S	C	V	C
M	S	G	J	I	F	I	B	J	Y

5 Complete the following sentences using the words below.

frequency   **medium**   **loudness**   **pitch**   **vacuum**

a   Sound cannot travel through a ....

b   Sound needs a .... to travel through, such as a solid or a liquid.

c   Blowing harder into a saxophone will increase the **amplitude** of the sound and its ....

d   A sound with more vibrations each second has a higher ....

e   The greater the **frequency** of a sound, the higher its ....

LANGUAGE FOCUS

To describe or predict how something will behave, use the first conditional. The first conditional includes the word *if*. You can begin the sentence with *if* or put it in the middle.

When you want to say that something is certain to happen, use *will (not)*. *Will (not)* needs another verb after it:

If you turn the volume control, the loudness of the sound <u>will increase</u> or decrease.

The loudness of the sound <u>will increase</u> or decrease <u>if</u> you turn the volume control.

When you want to say that something is possible but not certain, use might (not).

If you shout in a very large room, you <u>might hear</u> an echo.

Notice that the verb after *if* is in the present simple tense:

<u>If</u> the room <u>is</u> empty, the echo will be louder.

You might hear an echo <u>if</u> you <u>shout</u> in a very large room.

---

6   **Cathode ray oscilloscopes** can be used to 'see' sounds by showing them as a trace on a screen. Figure 12.2 shows a sound waveform. (Circle) the correct option to complete each sentence.

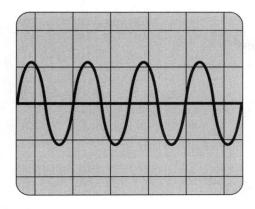

Figure 12.2: A sound wave shown on a cathode ray oscilloscope.

a If the loudness of the sound is increased, then the amplitude of the sound will *increase / decrease*.

b If the frequency of the sound decreases, then the number of waves shown on screen will *increase / decrease*

c If the pitch of the sound is low, then the frequency of the sound will be *high / low*.

d If the sound is quiet, then the amplitude of the sound will be *large / small*.

7 Figure 12.3 shows the sound wave of a piano on a **cathode ray oscilloscope**. Write the answers using the first conditional. Use the Language focus box to help you.

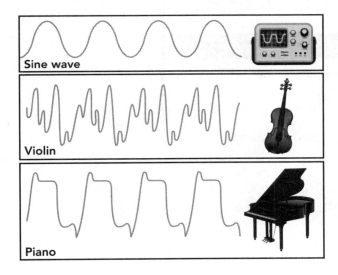

Figure 12.3: A sine wave and sound waves of a violin and a piano shown on a cathode ray oscilloscope.

a What will happen to the sound wave if its frequency increases?

....

b What will happen to the sound wave if its loudness decreases?

....

c Suggest what might happen to the sound wave if the sound travels a long distance in a concert hall.

....

....

Exercise 12.3 Range of hearing and speed of sound

IN THIS EXERCISE YOU WILL:

Science skills:

- describe the range of human hearing and what ultrasound is

- describe how to measure the speed of sound.

English skills:

- practise answering questions beginning with *how*

- practise giving instructions.

KEY WORDS

range of frequency: the difference between the highest and the lowest frequency

In this exercise, you will look at the **range of frequency** of sound that humans and other animals can hear and how to measure the speed of sound.

LANGUAGE FOCUS

You will often see questions beginning with *how* + adjective. A familiar example is *How old are you?* In physics, these questions often relate to distance, speed, frequency, etc.

How fast can a sound travel through a solid?

How far can a whale emit sounds to another whale?

The answer usually includes the adjective used in the question, or a measurement:

How <u>fast</u> can a sound travel through a solid?

A sound can travel through a solid very <u>fast</u>.

How far can a whale emit sounds to another whale?

About <u>800 km</u>.

Questions with *how* and the adverb *well* are also possible.

How well can a bat see?

How well can a bat hear?

8   Figure 12.4 shows the ranges of sound that can be heard by different animals. Match the question to the answer.

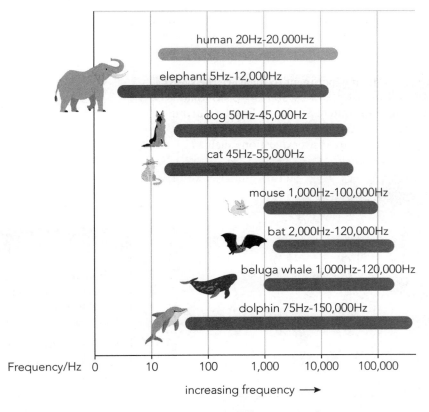

Figure 12.4: The ranges of sound heard by different animals.

Question	Answer
A How high a frequency of sound can humans hear?	**1** 120 000 Hz
B How low a frequency of sound can dogs hear?	**2** 20 000 Hz
C How high a frequency of sound can bats hear?	**3** 5 Hz
D How low a frequency of sound can elephants hear?	**4** 50 Hz

9 a What is ultrasound?

....

b Look at Figure 12.4. Which animals cannot hear ultrasound?

....

c Give two uses of ultrasound.

....

....

10 Figure 12.5 shows two students carrying out an experiment to measure the speed of sound. They are in a field with the following apparatus: starting pistol that produces a puff of smoke, hodometer and stopwatch. Student 1 has the starting pistol and student 2 has the stopwatch. Write instructions for the experiment. The first one has been done for you. Remember to answer questions such as *How far apart? How should the result be calculated?*

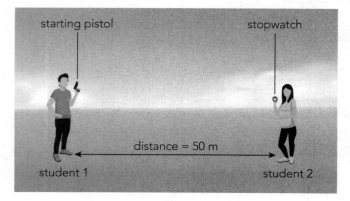

Figure 12.5: Experiment to find the speed of sound in air.

LANGUAGE TIP

When you explain a method, you often need the structure *Use (noun) to (verb)* …

For example: *Use this equation to calculate the speed.*

1   Use the trundle wheel to measure 50 m from student 1 to student 2.

2   ....

3   ....

4   ....

5   ....

Chapter 13
Light

Exercise 13.1 Reflection

KEY WORDS

reflection: the change of direction of a ray when it strikes the surface of a material without passing through it

laterally inverted: reversed left to right

ray diagram: a diagram showing the path of a ray of light

In this exercise, you will look at **reflection** of a light ray in a mirror and the type of image that is produced.

1 Match each key term with its definition.

Term	Definition
A reflected ray	**1** a line drawn at right angles to a surface
B incident ray	**2** the angle between the reflected ray and the normal
C angle of reflection	**3** a ray of light that arrives at a surface
D normal	**4** the angle between the incident ray and the normal
E angle of incidence	**5** a ray of light that bounces off a surface

2 Are the following statements about an image formed by a mirror true or false?

(Circle) the correct answers.

a The image is a different size to the object. *True / False*

b The image is **laterally inverted**. *True / False*

c The image is real and can be formed on a screen. *True / False*

d The distances between the mirror and the image and the mirror and the object are the same. *True / False*

3 **a** Figure 13.1 shows the reflection of a light ray from a plane mirror. Follow the instructions to complete the **ray diagram**.

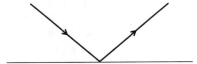

Figure 13.1: Ray diagram.

    i Label the mirror.

    ii Label the incident ray and the reflected ray.

    iii Draw the normal to the surface of the mirror at the point where the incident ray strikes it.

    iv Label the angle of incidence and the angle of reflection.

....

b State the law of reflection.

....

Exercise 13.2 Refraction

IN THIS EXERCISE YOU WILL:

Science skills:

- describe refraction of light

- describe total internal reflection.

English skills:

- practise using appropriate verbs and prepositions of movement.

KEY WORDS

refraction: the bending of light when it passes from one medium to another

critical angle: the minimum angle of incidence at which total internal reflection occurs

In this exercise, you will look at **refraction** of a light ray. Refraction occurs because light travels at different speeds in different materials.

LANGUAGE FOCUS

To describe refraction, you need to be able to use appropriate verbs and prepositions of movement.

Verbs:

bend   enter   leave   pass   travel

A light ray <u>travels</u> through the air in a straight line until it <u>enters</u> a different material.

As the light ray <u>leaves</u> the air, its path <u>bends</u>.

Enter and *leave* are followed by a noun:

The light ray <u>leaves the mirror</u> at an angle of 40°.

Prepositions:

bend, pass and *travel* are often used with prepositions of movement:

pass from / into / through   bend away from / towards

As light <u>passes into</u> a glass block, it <u>bends towards</u> the normal.

LANGUAGE TIP

After (doing) and having (done) mean the same thing. Use the *-ing* form with *after*, but the past participle after *having*:

<u>after travelling</u> through water = <u>having travelled</u> through water

<u>after leaving</u> = <u>having left</u>

4 Figure 13.2 shows a light ray travelling from air into glass. Complete these sentences using the correct prepositions. Use the words below. Words can be used more than once.

away from   from   into   through   towards

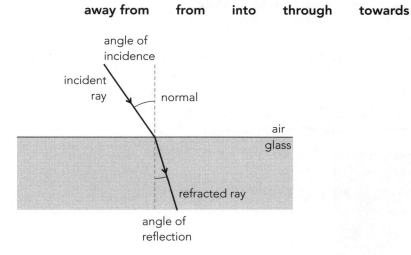

Figure 13.2: Refraction of light.

a After travelling .... air .... glass, a light ray refracts.

b When light enters glass, having been in air, it bends .... the normal.

c When light enters air, having been in glass, it bends .... the normal.

d Light can travel .... a glass window, but it cannot travel

.... a wall.

5 Figure 13.3 shows a ray of light travelling through a rectangular glass block. Answer the questions using complete sentences and appropriate verbs and prepositions.

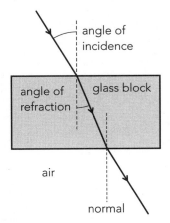

Figure 13.3: Light travelling through a glass block.

a Describe what happens to the light ray as it enters the glass block.

....

b Describe what happens to the light ray as it passes through the glass block.

....

c Describe what happens to the light ray as it leaves the glass block.

....

6 Figure 13.4 shows a light ray incident on a semicircular glass block. Explain what is happening to the light ray. Use the term **critical angle** in your explanation.

Figure 13.4: A light ray hitting a semicircular glass block.

....

....

....

....

Exercise 13.3 Lenses

IN THIS EXERCISE YOU WILL:

Science skills:

- describe how lenses form images and the types of images formed.

English skills:

- practise using key terms related to lenses
- use *as*, *before* and *after* to talk about light travelling through a lens.

KEY WORDS

principal focus: the point at which rays of light parallel to the principal axis converge after passing through a converging lens

In this exercise, you will look at lenses. Different lenses refract the light rays passing through them in different ways and produce different types of images.

7 Match each key term with its definition.

Term	Definition
A converging lens	1 the distance from the centre of a lens to its **principal focus**
B principal axis	2 a lens that causes light rays parallel to the principal axis to come together at the principal focus
C diverging lens	3 a line passing through the centre of a lens
D focal length	4 a lens that causes light rays parallel to the principal axis to spread out

LANGUAGE FOCUS

In physics, you often state if one action happens before, after, or at the same time as another action:

A metal block is heated. The volume of the block increases. (The two actions happen at the same time.)

A switch closes a circuit. The bell rings. (The circuit is closed, then the bell rings.)

You can express these ideas using *before, after* or *as.*

Use *as* + verb phrase to express two actions occurring at the same time. If one of the actions is the direct result of the other action, use as in front of the cause, not the result:

<u>*As a metal block is heated*</u>*, it expands.*

A metal block expands <u>*as it is heated*</u>*.*

Before and *after* can also be used with a verb clause:

<u>*Before the bell rings*</u>*, the switch closes the circuit.*

The switch closes the circuit <u>*before the bell rings*</u>*.*

<u>*After the switch closes*</u> *the circuit, the bell rings.*

The bell rings <u>*after the switch closes the circuit*</u>*.*

When you start a sentence with *as, after* or *before,* there is a comma before the second action.

If both actions are done by the same person or thing, you can use *before / after* + *-ing* or *before / after* + noun:

<u>*Before carrying*</u> *out the experiment, we set up the equipment.*

<u>*After the equipment*</u> *was set up, we carried out the experiment.*

8   Figure 13.5 shows what happens when light rays travel through a converging lens. Answer the questions with full sentences and use the words *before, after* and *as.*

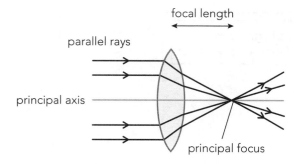

Figure 13.5: Light rays travelling through a converging lens.

a   Describe the light rays before they reach the converging lens.

....

b   What happens to the light rays as they pass through the lens?

....

c   What happens to the light rays after they pass through the lens?

....

9   a   Draw a labelled ray diagram for a converging lens. The focal length of the lens is 5 cm. The object is 2 cm tall and is 10 cm from the lens. Draw the diagram to scale.

> **LANGUAGE TIP**
>
> In science, you usually have to draw diagrams to scale. This means that all measurements need to be proportional, e.g. $\frac{1}{10}$ of the original measurements.

b   What type of image is formed by the converging lens in the ray diagram you have drawn?

....

Chapter 14
Properties of waves

IN THIS CHAPTER YOU WILL:

Science skills:

- describe the properties of waves and the differences between transverse and longitudinal waves
- describe reflection, refraction and diffraction of waves.

English skills:

- recognise and use open and closed question forms
- practise using sequencers and conjunctions.

Exercise 14.1 Describing waves

IN THIS EXERCISE YOU WILL:

Science skills:

- describe the properties of waves
- interpret graphs used to represent waves.

English skills:

- practise using key vocabulary used to describe waves.

KEY WORDS

period: the time taken for one complete wave to pass a particular point

ripple tank: a shallow water tank used to demonstrate how waves behave

In this exercise, you will look at the properties of waves and interpret graphs used to represent waves.

1   Find eight words for describing waves in the word string and write them on the lines below. One has been done for you.

crestwavelengthhertzperiodfrequencytroughamplitudespeed

crest ....

....

....

....

2   Fill in the gaps to complete the sentences. Use the words below. Words can be used more than once.

crest   frequency   period   wavelength

a   The highest point of a wave is the ....

b   The .... of a wave is the distance between two crests or two troughs that are next to each other.

c   The .... of a wave is the time it takes for one complete wave to pass a particular point.

d   The number of waves passing a particular point per second is the

    ....

e   Waves with a long **period** have a low ....

f   The equation for wave speed is: wave speed = frequency ×

    ....

3   Figure 14.1 shows a graph of a water wave in a **ripple tank**.

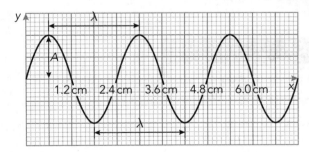

Figure 14.1: A graph of a water wave in a ripple tank.

a   The *y*-axis shows the displacement of the water. What quantity is shown on the *x*-axis?

    ....

b   Which quantities are represented by the following symbols:

    i   *A* ....

    ii *λ* ....

c   The frequency of the water wave is 18 Hz. Calculate the period of the wave.

    ....

d   i   Look at Figure 14.1. What is the wavelength of the water wave?

        ....

    ii Calculate the speed of the water wave.

        ....

Exercise 14.2 Transverse waves and longitudinal waves

IN THIS EXERCISE YOU WILL:

Science skills:

- describe the differences between transverse waves and longitudinal waves.

English skills:

- recognise and use open and closed question forms
- practise using sequencers to indicate the order that events happen.

KEY WORDS

rarefaction: a region where the particles of the wave are closer together

In this exercise, you will look at the differences between transverse waves and longitudinal waves.

LANGUAGE FOCUS

There are two different types of question: closed questions and open questions. You can identify the type of question from the first word in the question.

The first word in a closed question is a 'short' verb, called an auxiliary:

Can   Does   Did   Is   Are   Were   Would   Will

The subject comes immediately after the auxiliary:

Can you use a tablet for this?

Will the sound get louder?

The answer to a closed question is yes or no.

The first word in an open question is usually a question word, for example, _what, which, where_ or _how_, but not always. Open questions can be formed in different ways.

preposition + _what / which_ + noun:

At what point ...?   _On which axis ...?_

How + adjective:

How long ...?   _How loud ...?_

How much / many + noun:

How many points ...?   _How much energy ...?_

For all forms, an auxiliary comes next, then a subject:

At what frequency do we begin to hear sound?

Why do _waves_ refract?

The answer to an open question is a piece of information.

4   Are the following questions open or closed? Circle the correct answers.

    a   Does a wave transfer energy and not matter from one place to another? _Open / Closed_

    b   What is the peak of a wave? _Open / Closed_

    c   How is the wavelength of a wave shown on a graph? _Open / Closed_

    d   Is the frequency of a wave the number of waves that passes a point in one second? _Open / Closed_

5   Darius models a longitudinal wave and a transverse wave on a slinky spring

Figure 14.2: Longitudinal wave and a transverse wave on a slinky spring.

a   Put the correct label (transverse or longitudinal) under each picture.

b   Fill in the gaps in the sentences describing the differences between transverse waves and longitudinal waves. Use the words below. Words can be used more than once.

compressions   longitudinal   transverse   troughs

In a .... wave, the particles move from side to side, at

right angles to the direction of travel of the wave. In a ....
wave, the particles move forwards and backwards, along the direction of

travel of the wave. A transverse wave has peaks and ....

A longitudinal wave has .... and **rarefactions**.

Electromagnetic waves are .... waves. Sound waves are

.... waves.

> **LANGUAGE TIP**
>
> When you describe a process or an experiment, use sequencers to indicate the order that things happen, such as: *initially, first, first of all, after that, next, then* and *finally*. Sequencers come at the start of a sentence and are usually followed by a comma.

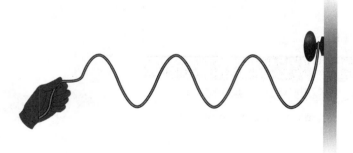

Figure 14.3: Transverse wave on a piece of rope.

6   Describe how you can model a transverse wave on a piece of rope and how you can increase the amplitude and then the frequency of the waves. Use sequencers in your description.

....

....

....

....

....

....

Exercise 14.3 Reflection, refraction and diffraction

IN THIS EXERCISE YOU WILL:

Science skills:

*   describe reflection, refraction and diffraction of waves.

English skills:

*   practise *causing* + noun + *to* verb and *therefore* in explanations.

KEY WORDS

diffraction: when a wave spreads out as it travels through a gap or past the edge of an object

In this exercise, you will look at how all waves can undergo reflection, refraction and **diffraction**.

7 The table shows pictures of different wave phenomena. Complete the table to show whether the phenomenon is reflection, refraction or diffraction. Use the Language tip box to help you.

Phenomenon	Picture
	 Figure 14.4a
	 Figure 14.4b
	 Figure 14.4c

8 Figure 14.5 shows a ripple tank. A ripple tank can be used to demonstrate

reflection, refraction and diffraction of water waves. (Circle) the correct word to complete each sentence.

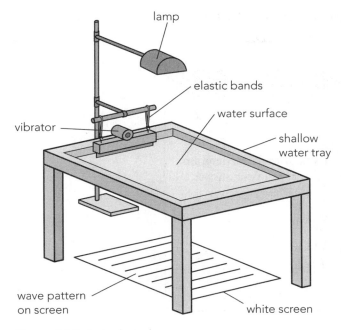

Figure 14.5: A ripple tank.

a   When water waves travel from deep water to shallow water, they slow down, causing the waves to *refract / diffract*.

b   When water waves pass through a gap, they *diffract / reflect*, causing them to spread out.

c   Water waves are *refracted / reflected* when they hit a barrier, causing them to overlap.

9   Figure 14.6 shows a water wave going from deep water to shallow water. Answer each question using the following structure: *[Observation]. Therefore, we can say that [answer]*. Use the Language tip box to help you.

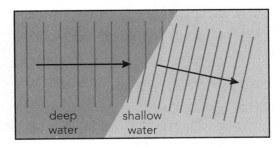

Figure 14.6: Water wave going from deep water to shallow water.

a   How does the diagram show the wavelength of the wave decreasing as it enters the shallow water?

....

LANGUAGE TIP

Use *causing* + noun + *to* verb as an alternative to *so that* + noun + verb phrase. This is formal English, frequently used in science.

When white light waves pass through a glass block, they change speed, <u>causing a spectrum to form</u>.

LANGUAGE TIP

You can use the word *therefore* to explain an answer:

The line on the graph goes up steeply. <u>Therefore</u>, we can say that the car was travelling at high speed.

b The frequency of the wave stays the same but the wavelength decreases. What happens to the speed of the wave?

....

c The wave bends as it enters the shallow water. What wave phenomenon does this show?

....

10 Figure 14.7 shows waves travelling through two gaps. Explain what the diagram shows. Use *[Observation]. Therefore, we can say that [answer]* in your answer. Use the Language tip box to help you.

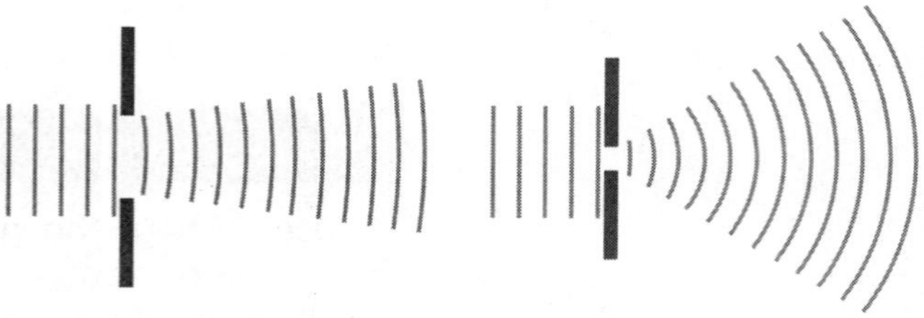

Figure 14.7: Waves travelling through two gaps.

....

....

....

....

....

....

Chapter 15

The electromagnetic spectrum

IN THIS CHAPTER YOU WILL:

Science skills:

- describe the electromagnetic spectrum and the properties of its waves
- describe uses and hazards of electromagnetic waves.

English skills:

- express position using prepositions
- practise using *can* and *may* in the passive form and verbs in the past simple.

Exercise 15.1 The electromagnetic spectrum

IN THIS EXERCISE YOU WILL:

Science skills:

- describe the electromagnetic spectrum and the properties of its waves.

English skills:

- express position using prepositions.

KEY WORDS

electromagnetic spectrum: the spectrum of all the wavelengths of electromagnetic waves

In this exercise, you will look at the waves in the **electromagnetic spectrum** and their properties. The electromagnetic spectrum ranges from radio waves, which have the longest wavelength, to gamma rays, which have the shortest wavelength.

1   Find the names of the seven forms of electromagnetic waves in the electromagnetic spectrum in the word search.

M	G	N	O	G	A	Y	V	R	N	H	J	P	I	T	M	D	J
I	M	O	P	A	V	I	S	I	B	L	E	G	S	O	U	F	C
C	F	W	W	Q	L	V	E	E	X	S	K	I	H	S	J	Z	S
R	U	B	F	V	Z	L	I	E	Z	M	N	N	A	H	L	M	C
O	R	A	D	I	O	Z	H	A	G	A	M	M	A	A	W	Y	R
W	Y	T	S	V	B	K	T	H	K	G	D	I	O	P	R	Z	H
A	U	L	T	R	A	V	I	O	L	E	T	L	V	K	G	W	K
V	O	Q	S	S	H	D	K	C	Z	V	X	D	T	M	Y	J	A
E	S	T	T	E	T	W	O	R	Y	W	R	Z	F	M	F	U	R
S	V	Y	N	A	S	C	T	C	X	S	A	U	B	W	T	N	M
I	N	F	R	A	R	E	D	V	O	A	Y	O	R	V	Y	Q	N
A	V	F	Q	X	I	K	J	O	E	Z	M	X	G	R	M	E	J

2   Fill in the gaps to complete the sentences about electromagnetic waves. Use the words below. Not all of the words need to be used. Words can be used more than once.

decreases   frequency   increases   speed
transverse   wavelength

a   Electromagnetic waves are .... waves.

b   Electromagnetic waves travel at the same .... in a vacuum, so as the frequency of a wave increases, its wavelength ....

c   The different colours in the spectrum of visible light depend on the .... of the waves.

d   Red light has a longer .... than violet light.

LANGUAGE FOCUS

To give accurate descriptions of position, use prepositions and expressions of position. Useful prepositions and expressions include:

between (with something on each side):

Orange is <u>between</u> red and yellow in the visible light spectrum.

beyond (after, further away than, at a greater distance than):

Humans cannot see electromagnetic waves <u>beyond</u> violet in the visible light spectrum.

towards (near, closer to):

The wavelength decreases as we move from red light <u>towards</u> violet light.

Note: Different versions of English use different spellings. For example, you might see *towards* in UK English and *toward* in US English. They are both correct.

in the region of (in the area around):

Visible light is found in the region of the spectrum between 10^{13} Hz and 10^{15} Hz.

3   Answer the questions about the electromagnetic spectrum using prepositions and expressions of position. Write complete sentences.

a   Where is yellow light found in the spectrum of visible light?

   ....

b   Where are radio waves in the electromagnetic spectrum?

   ....

c   The wavelength increases from infrared to microwaves. What happens to the frequency?

   ....

d   Where can X-rays be found in the electromagnetic spectrum?

   ....

Exercise 15.2 Uses of electromagnetic waves

IN THIS EXERCISE YOU WILL:

Science skills:

- describe uses of electromagnetic waves.

English skills:

- practise using *can* and *may* in the passive form.

KEY WORDS

short range communication: wireless communication over a very short distance

The waves in the electromagnetic spectrum have different wavelengths / frequencies. This gives them different properties. In this exercise, you will look at some of the uses of the different waves.

4   Write the waves of the electromagnetic spectrum in order of increasing frequency with the lowest frequency at the top. The first one has been done for you.

radio waves
....

....

....

....

....

....

....

LANGUAGE FOCUS

Remember, the passive form is made using the verb *be* with the past participle:

In this experiment, light is <u>refracted</u>.

However, you can also use *can* and *may* with the passive, to suggest ability (*can*) and possibility (*may*). Make the passive with *can* or *may* in the same way:

can / may (not) + be + past participle

Ultraviolet light can be seen by some birds. (Can expresses ability.)

Ultraviolet light may be seen by some other animals. (May expresses possibility.)

The general rule is:

- for ability: use *can*

- for possibility: use *may*.

Sometimes you use *by* to introduce the person or thing doing the action. You do this when the person or thing is important but not the main focus of the text:

Ultraviolet light was discovered by Johann W Ritter. (A sentence about ultraviolet light.)

Johann W Ritter discovered ultraviolet light. (A sentence about Johann W Ritter.)

5   Are these statements about uses of electromagnetic waves true or false? Tick (✓) the correct box in the table.

Statement	True	False
Infrared may be used to sterilise water.		
Radio waves can be used for broadcasting TV signals.		
Gamma rays may be used to heat food.		
Ultraviolet can be used to detect forged bank notes.		
X-rays can be used in security scanners at airports.		
Microwaves may be used in remote controls.		

LANGUAGE TIP

Can is often found in the passive form in the expression *X can be used to* (verb):

A glass of water <u>can be used to</u> refract light.

6   Complete the sentences with *can be* or *cannot be*.

Radio waves and microwaves .... used for communications. Radio

waves .... used for **short range communication**, such as Bluetooth.

Infrared .... be used to detect metal objects hidden inside baggage.

Infrared .... used to cook food in grills and toasters. Gamma

rays .... used to cook food as they are not absorbed by the water

molecules in the food. Gamma rays .... used to kill cancer cells.

Ultraviolet .... used to help humans to see in the dark.

7   Write about the uses of three electromagnetic waves. Use the passive form and *can* or *may*.

....

....

....

....

....

....

Exercise 15.3 Hazards of electromagnetic waves

IN THIS EXERCISE YOU WILL:

Science skills:

•   describe hazards of electromagnetic waves.

English skills:

•   practise using verbs in the past simple tense.

KEY WORDS

hazard: something that could potentially cause someone harm or cause them to become ill

In this exercise, you will look at the **hazards** of electromagnetic waves and how electromagnetic waves can be used safely.

LANGUAGE FOCUS

The past simple tense is used to describe actions in the past. The active form is used when the person or thing carrying out the action is known and important in the context:

We placed the prism on a flat surface. We checked the surfaces of the prism were clean.

It can also be used with sequencers or linkers:

First, we placed the prism on a flat surface and we checked that the surfaces of the prism were clean.

The past simple active is easy to form:

- For regular verbs, add -*ed* to the verb: *check – checked.*
- If the verb ends with an *e*, add -*d* to the verb: place – *placed.*
- If the verb ends with a consonant and -*y*, change the -*y* to -*i*: *carry – carried.*

For irregular verbs, look for their past form in a verb table:

find – found   go – went

Most verbs have only one past simple form. *Be* is the only verb that has two forms:

was (I, it, he, she): The prism was clean.

were (we, you, they): The surfaces were clean.

For the negative form: use *did not* + verb:

They did not understand the results.

We did not see all the colours clearly.

Be is irregular in the negative:

The surface was not flat.

The colours were not all clear.

8   Complete the table with the past simple forms and state if the verbs are regular or
    irregular. One has been done for you.

Verb	Past simple form	Regular or irregular?
to choose	chose	irregular
to pass		
to compare		
to measure		
to apply		
to place		
to shine		

9   Fill in the gaps to complete the sentences about the hazards of electromagnetic
    waves. Use the words below. Not all of the words will be needed.

       frequency   gamma rays   infrared   microwaves

                ultraviolet   wavelength

Most electromagnetic waves can be harmful to humans. The greater the

.... of a wave, the more dangerous it can be. ....
radiation from the Sun can cause damage to skin and eye cells. If large amounts

of .... are absorbed, they can cause cells inside the body to

heat up. X-rays and .... are the most dangerous forms of
electromagnetic waves. They can cause cells to mutate, which can lead to cancer.

10 Thomas works as a radiographer in a hospital and took an X-ray of a patient.
    Write about how he protected himself from the hazards of using X-rays. Use the
    past simple and the active or passive form as appropriate. Use the Language tip
    box to help you.

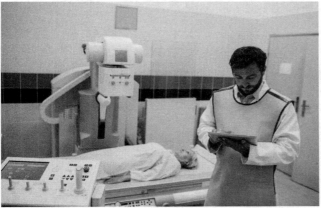

Figure 15.1: Taking an X-ray.

....

....

....

....

> Chapter 16
Magnetism

Exercise 16.1 Magnetic forces

KEY WORDS

north pole: the magnetic pole of a magnet that points towards the Earth's North Pole

bar magnet: a rectangular permanent magnet with a north pole at one end and a south pole at the other end

south pole: the magnetic pole of a magnet that points towards the Earth's South Pole

In this exercise, you will look at magnetic forces and the differences between hard and soft magnetic materials.

1   Find seven terms related to magnetism in the word string. Write them on the lines below. One has been done for you.

barmagnetmagnetisednorthpoleattractionunmagnetisedsouthpolerepulsion

bar magnet ....

....

....

....

....

....

....

2   Word families are groups of nouns, verbs and adjectives that are related to each other. Complete the table using the words below.

attraction   attractive   magnet   magnetise   repel   repulsive

Adjective	Noun	Verb
		attract
	repulsion	
magnetic		

3   Complete the sentences using the correct form of the words in question **2**.

a   There is an .... force between the **north pole** of one **bar magnet** and the **south pole** of another bar magnet. The north pole of one magnet

.... the south pole of the other magnet.

b   The north pole of one magnet .... the north pole of another

magnet. There is a force of .... between them.

c   You can .... a piece of iron by rubbing it with a strong

.... When it is ...., it can be used to magnetise a steel pin by induced magnetism.

4   Explain the difference between hard magnetic materials and soft magnetic materials. Use appropriate nouns, verbs and adjectives in your answer.

....

....

....

....

Exercise 16.2 Magnetic fields

IN THIS EXERCISE YOU WILL:

Science skills:

- describe magnetic fields and magnetic field lines.

English skills:

- practise using prepositions.

KEY WORDS

magnetic field lines: lines that represent the direction the magnetic force would have on the north pole of a magnet

magnetic field: the region of space around a magnet or electric current in which a magnetic pole experiences a force

plotting compass: a small compass with a needle that lines up with magnetic field lines

In this exercise, you will look at how **magnetic field lines** are used to represent the **magnetic field** around a magnet.

5 Figure 16.1 shows the magnetic field lines around a bar magnet. Complete the diagram by drawing arrows on the field lines to show their direction.

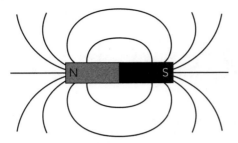

Figure 16.1: Magnetic field lines around a bar magnet.

6 Complete the sentences about magnetic field lines with the prepositions below. There may be more than one possible answer for each.

away from   from   into   out of   to   towards

a Magnetic field lines are always shown as coming .... a magnetic north pole.

b The north pole of a magnet points .... the Earth's geographical North Pole.

c A magnetic north pole and a magnetic south pole are attracted

.... each other.

d If two magnetic north poles are brought together, they will repel

.... each other.

e You always show magnetic field lines as going .... a magnetic south pole.

7   Write a paragraph describing how to plot magnetic field lines around a bar magnet using a **plotting compass**. Use prepositions in your answer.

....

....

....

....

....

....

....

....

....

Exercise 16.3 Electromagnets

IN THIS EXERCISE YOU WILL:

Science skills:

- describe electromagnets and their uses.

English skills:

- practise using key vocabulary related to electromagnets.

KEY WORDS

electromagnet: a coil of wire that acts as a magnet when an electric current passes through it

In this exercise, you will look at how **electromagnets** are produced and what they are used for.

8 Find ten terms in the word search related to electromagnets.

M	M	I	P	C	S	N	N	L	S	I	N	E	A
A	U	N	P	H	W	O	I	O	O	N	S	E	I
G	O	B	C	I	E	R	O	M	U	T	E	G	R
N	O	A	O	N	L	T	L	O	T	T	O	T	O
E	O	R	S	R	L	H	N	N	H	N	R	L	N
T	T	M	O	L	W	P	W	E	P	E	R	N	C
I	G	A	L	S	O	O	O	N	O	R	N	A	O
C	O	G	E	W	T	L	E	N	L	R	C	R	R
F	O	N	N	I	I	E	T	N	E	U	N	O	E
I	I	E	O	S	R	R	I	I	B	C	L	C	I
E	A	T	I	C	A	E	E	P	A	C	O	I	L
L	L	N	D	I	D	E	U	E	R	R	I	I	D
D	T	E	N	G	A	M	O	R	T	C	E	L	E
E	E	T	O	I	E	W	N	E	E	E	I	A	R

9 **a** Fill in the gaps to complete the sentences about electromagnets.
Use the words below.

bar magnet   coil   electric current   magnetic field   solenoid

An electromagnet is made from a .... of wire, known as

a .... When an .... passes through it, a

.... is produced around it, similar to the one around a

....

b Give the three ways that the strength of an electromagnet can be increased.

....

....

....

10 Figure 16.2 shows an electromagnetic crane used in a scrap yard. Explain how and why an electromagnet is used to pick up the metal scrap.

Figure 16.2: An electromagnetic crane.

....

....

....

....

Chapter 17

Static electricity

IN THIS CHAPTER YOU WILL:

Science skills:

- describe static electricity and the two types of electrostatic charge

- describe the difference between electrical conductors and insulators.

English skills:

- practice using the passive form and past participles

- practice using *can* and the *-ing* form of verbs.

Exercise 17.1 Electrostatic charges

IN THIS EXERCISE YOU WILL:

Science skills:

- describe electrostatic charges.

English skills:

- recognise descriptions, observations and explanations

- practise using the passive form and past participles.

KEY WORDS

electrostatic charge: a property of an object that causes it to attract or repel other objects with charge

In this exercise, you will look at the two types of **electrostatic charge**, positive charge and negative charge, and the forces that two charges exert on each other.

1 Match the sentence halves to complete the sentences about electrostatic charge.

A A positive charge is...	**1** ...repel each other
B A negative charge and a positive charge will...	**2** ...the type of charge carried by an electron
C A negative charge is...	**3** ...attract each other
D Two negative charges will...	**4** ...the overall charge of the nucleus of an atom

> **LANGUAGE TIP**
>
> When you write about experiments, you need to use three types of statement:
>
> • descriptions that tell you *how* it was done
>
> • observations that tell you *what* happened
>
> • explanations that tell you *why* it happened.

2 Figure 17.1 shows an experiment to investigate electrostatic charge. Read each statement below, then (circle) D, O or E to show whether it is a description (D), an observation (O) or an explanation (E).

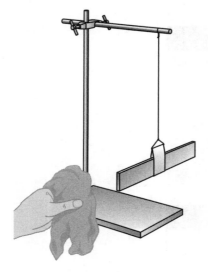

Figure 17.1: Experiment to investigate electrostatic charge.

a A plastic rod is hung from a clamp stand using thread so that it is free to move. *D / O / E*

b One end of the rod is rubbed with a cloth. *D / O / E*

c When the cloth is brought close to the rod, the rod moves towards the cloth. *D / O / E*

d Rubbing the rod gives it a negative charge. *D / O / E*

e The cloth is left with a positive charge. *D / O / E*

f The rod moves because opposite charges are attracted towards each other. *D / O / E*

LANGUAGE FOCUS

When you write about experiments, you use the passive. This means you need to be familiar with the past participles of verbs such as *hang*, *record*, *place* and *observe*:

A plastic rod *is hung* using thread.

The results *are recorded*.

The charged rod *is placed* near another charged rod.

Changes *are observed*.

3 **a** Complete the table by writing the missing verbs and past participles.

Verb	Past participle
rub	rubbed
attract	
bring	
	hung
show	
charge	
	left
move	

b Rewrite each sentence using the passive and past participles.

i I collected my equipment.

....

ii I set up the equipment in the way the diagram showed.

....

iii I rubbed the plastic rod with the cloth.

....

iv I brought the cloth near the plastic rod.

....

4 Harpreet carries out an experiment to demonstrate electrostatic charge. She has a cloth, a plastic rod and small pieces of paper. Write about her experiment, using the passive and past participles.

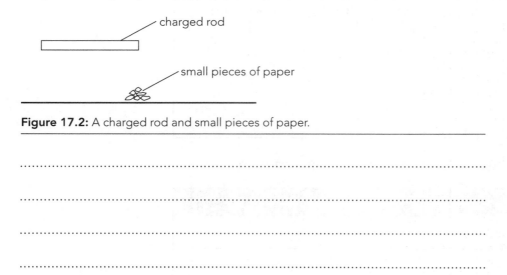

Figure 17.2: A charged rod and small pieces of paper.

....

....

....

....

Exercise 17.2 Explaining static electricity

IN THIS EXERCISE YOU WILL:

Science skills:

- explain static electricity

- describe the difference between electrical conductors and electrical insulators.

English skills:

- practise using *can*.

KEY WORDS

electrical conductor: a material that allows the flow of electrons (electric current)

electrical insulator: a material that does not allow the flow of electrons (electric current)

In this exercise, you will look at how static electricity is generated and the difference between **electrical conductors** and **electrical insulators**.

5   Find thirteen words in the word search to do with static electricity.

F	X	S	H	O	W	C	Z	F	V	E	B	P	I	N
D	T	O	Q	R	V	R	O	K	D	I	V	R	N	O
M	U	S	N	V	J	I	Y	N	C	O	G	O	S	I
E	V	I	T	A	G	E	N	P	D	W	L	T	U	T
E	N	L	O	D	G	B	O	J	T	U	L	O	L	C
M	I	O	Z	D	B	S	C	R	G	A	C	N	A	I
J	H	W	R	Q	I	N	C	Z	R	H	V	T	T	R
E	L	E	C	T	R	O	S	T	A	T	I	C	O	F
N	S	A	I	O	C	B	U	R	L	E	P	E	R	R
D	E	V	T	N	K	E	G	N	E	U	T	R	O	N
T	E	O	T	T	N	E	L	X	S	G	Z	H	Q	V
V	M	C	P	D	R	U	T	E	D	N	E	J	H	F
Q	J	D	F	E	N	A	S	M	O	X	E	R	V	B
D	T	R	L	N	I	F	C	F	D	U	C	D	C	Z
P	T	B	Y	J	W	Y	B	T	Y	F	R	M	Z	O

6   Fill in the gaps to explain why a balloon sticks to a jumper when they are rubbed together. Use the words below. Not all the words need to be used.

       attract   **charge**   **conductors**   **electrons**   **insulators**
              positive   **negative**   **repel**

Both the balloon and the jumper are .... To begin with, they have

no .... so they are uncharged. When they are rubbed together,

friction causes .... to be transferred between the jumper and the

balloon. The object that gains them becomes .... and the object

that loses them becomes .... The balloon and the jumper now

have opposite charges and so they ....

LANGUAGE FOCUS

You have already seen that *can* is used to express ability. It can also be used to express possibility. It can be used in different ways:

can + verb:

You <u>can cause</u> static charge by rubbing a balloon on a sweater. *(expressing ability)*

Static charge <u>can make</u> your hair stand up. (expressing possibility)

When you use it to express possibility, the meaning is similar to *sometimes*.

Static charge <u>can make</u> your hair stand up. = Static charge <u>sometimes makes</u> your hair stand up.

can + be + past participle:

The paper <u>can be held</u> by using a drawing pin.

Static electricity <u>can be felt</u> when someone gets out of a car and gets a shock when they touch the door.

The passive form with *can* is often used in science. It is useful for descriptions and observations.

subject + can + use + object + to (verb):

<u>You can use a cloth to</u> charge a plastic rod.

You cannot use *can* in the future tense. If you need to express ability in the future, use:

will be able to + verb:

After you rub a balloon on your sweater, you <u>will be able to stick</u> the balloon to the ceiling.

7 Write a paragraph to explain the difference between electrical conductors and electrical insulators and why electrical conductors can become charged. Use *can* in your explanation.

....

....

....

....

....

....

Exercise 17.3 Electric fields

IN THIS EXERCISE YOU WILL:

Science skills:

- describe electric fields around charges.

English skills:

- practise using the *-ing* form of verbs.

KEY WORDS

lines of force: a way to represent force in an electric field

In this exercise, you will look at electric fields around charges and how they are represented.

8 Fill in the gaps to complete the sentences about charged objects. Use the words below. Words can be used more than once.

charged object   **electric field**   **force**   **touching**

There is an .... around a charged object. If you place another

.... in this field then it will experience a .... on it.

This means that a .... can affect another charged object without

.... it.

LANGUAGE FOCUS

The -ing form of verbs is often used in English. You can use the -ing form with am, are or is to describe what is or was happening. Many adjectives end in -ing. If you want to use a verb (to plot, to measure, to record) as a noun, add -ing:

plotting data   measuring the wavelength   recording the results

Use the -ing form of the verb if you can substitute the verb with a noun.

As the subject or object of the sentence:

Learning about electricity is fun.   I like learning about electricity.

After prepositions:

We learned about generating static electricity.

After some verbs:

stop, start, avoid, keep, enjoy, delay, involve, finish, remember

Stop recording the data.

Note: keep + -ing means continue + -ing.

9   Rewrite the following sentences using the -ing form. Use the Language focus box to help you.

   a   If you rub a plastic rod with a cloth, this gives the rod a negative charge.

   ....

   b   A charged object and an uncharged object do not need to touch for the uncharged object to experience a force.

   ....

   c   Any charged object that moves into an electric field experiences a force.

   ....

10 Figure 17.3 shows the **lines of force** around two charged objects.

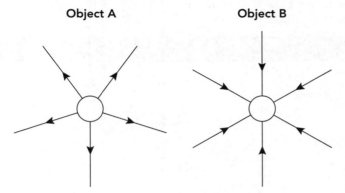

Figure 17.3: Lines of force around two charged objects.

a   Which object is negatively charged? Explain how you know it is
negatively charged.

....

....

....

b   Figure 17.4 shows two parallel charged plates. Complete the diagram by
drawing the lines of force.

Figure 17.4: Two parallel charged plates.

Chapter 18

Electrical quantities

IN THIS CHAPTER YOU WILL:

Science skills:

- describe current, potential difference and resistance
- describe electrical energy, work and power.

English skills:

- practise using articles and selecting the correct article
- practise using the second conditional.

Exercise 18.1 Electric current

IN THIS EXERCISE YOU WILL:

Science skills:

- describe current and how it can be measured.

English skills:

- practise using articles and selecting the correct article.

KEY WORDS

cell: a device that provides an electromotive force in a circuit

series circuit: a circuit where all the components are connected in a line with each other and the power source

In this exercise, you will look at what electric current is and how to measure it in an electric circuit.

1 Match each key term with its definition.

Term	Definition
A current	**1** current that flows in the same direction all the time
B alternating current	**2** what is carried around a circuit by the current
C ammeter	**3** the flow of electric charge
D conductor	**4** current that constantly changes direction
E direct current	**5** the unit of electric current
F charge	**6** a material that lets current flow through it
G ampere	**7** an instrument for measuring current

LANGUAGE FOCUS

The first time you refer to a singular countable noun, use *a / an*. After that, use *the*:

A circuit was set up. A lightbulb was then connected to the circuit.

Using *a* or *an* depends on the first sound in the word that follows it. If the sound is a consonant sound, use *a*:

a magnet   a good electrical conductor   a universal law

If it is a vowel sound, use *an*:

an ammeter   an hour   an effective conductor

2 Complete the sentences about an electric circuit using *a, an* or *the*.

.... electric circuit has .... **cell**, ...
switch and .... lamp. .... wires in
.... electric circuit are often made of copper because copper
is .... good electrical conductor. When ....
switch is closed, current flows around .... circuit. You can
use .... ammeter to measure .... current in
.... electrical circuit. If .... switch is not closed,
then no current will flow around .... circuit.

> **LANGUAGE TIP**
>
> *No* is not only the opposite of yes. It is also used before nouns to express *zero quantity*:
>
> *The circuit has <u>no</u> current flowing around it.* (The circuit has *zero current* flowing around it.)

3 Figure 18.1 shows an analogue ammeter. Answer the questions, using complete sentences and the correct articles.

Figure 18.1: An analogue ammeter.

a What is the reading on the ammeter? Give the unit.

....

b What is the difference between an analogue ammeter and a digital ammeter?

....

....

c Where should an ammeter be placed in a **series circuit** to measure the current?

....

Exercise 18.2 Potential difference and resistance

KEY WORDS

potential difference: the work done by a unit charge passing through an electrical component

resistance: a measure of how difficult it is for an electric current to flow through a device or a component in a circuit

e.m.f.: the electrical work done by a source (cell, battery, etc.) in moving (a unit) charge around a circuit

In this exercise, you will look at **potential difference** and **resistance** and what affects the resistance of a wire.

4   Find the seven key terms in the word string and write them on the lines below. The first one has been done for you.

voltageresistancevoltmeterohmelectromotiveforcevoltpotentialdifference

voltage
....

....

....

....

....

....

....

LANGUAGE FOCUS

In physics, you sometimes need to talk about a hypothetical situation. For example, measuring your mass on the Moon or being hit by lightning. To do this, use the second conditional. Make the second conditional by using *if* + past simple and *would* (*not*) + verb:

If you <u>measured</u> your mass on the Moon, it <u>would be</u> the same as on the Earth.

That tall house <u>would be</u> safer <u>if</u> there <u>was</u> a lighting conductor near it.

The passive form is also possible in the second conditional. In the passive form, you need two verbs after *if* and three verbs in the other part of the sentence.

If the length of a wire <u>were increased</u>, its resistance <u>would be increased</u>.

Although the past simple form of *be* with *it* (*he / she / I*) is *was*, you sometimes see *if it* (*he / she / I*) *were* in the second conditional. It is good scientific style to use *were* (not *was*) for *be* with singular and plural subjects in the second conditional:

That tall house <u>would be</u> safer if there <u>were</u> a lightning conductor near it.

Notice that, although you use the past simple, the second conditional does not refer to the past, but to all time. Look at the example sentences above – are they always true?

5   Complete the sentences by matching the sentence halves.

A If you increased the **e.m.f.** of a power supply in a circuit…	**1** …their e.m.fs would add together.
B If a longer wire were used in a circuit…	**2** …the current flowing around the circuit would increase.
C If you added cells in series…	**3** …the current flowing through the component would be decreased.
D If the resistance of a component were increased…	**4** …its resistance would be increased.

6 Figure 18.2 shows a circuit to measure the resistance of a wire.

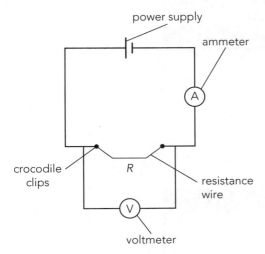

Figure 18.2: Circuit to measure the resistance of a wire.

a Answer the questions using full sentences and the second conditional.
Use the Language focus box to help you.

i What would happen to the resistance if the thickness of the wire
were increased?

....

ii What would be the effect of connecting the voltmeter in series with
the wire?

....

iii Describe what will happen to the current if the resistance of the wire was
decreased.

....

b The potential difference is 12 V and the current is 2.5 A. Calculate the
resistance of the wire. Give the unit.

....

Exercise 18.3 Energy and power

IN THIS EXERCISE YOU WILL:

Science skills:

- describe electrical energy and electrical power.

English skills:

- practise using different expressions for introducing examples.

KEY WORDS

power rating: the maximum amount of energy that an appliance transfers per second when the appliance is being used

In this exercise, you will look at the transfer of electrical energy in an electrical circuit and what electrical power is.

7 Are these statements true or false? (Circle) the correct answer.

   a The e.m.f. of a power supply is the amount of energy it transfers to charges flowing around an electric circuit. *True / False*

   b The smaller the current flowing around a circuit, the faster the energy is transferred. *True / False*

   c The equation for electrical energy is: $E = IRt$. *True / False*

   d Electrical power is a measure of the rate at which electrical energy is transferred. *True / False*

LANGUAGE FOCUS

There are a variety of connectives and expressions that you can use for introducing examples. The best ones are:

for example   *for instance*   *such as*

For example and *for instance* can be used at the start of a sentence followed by a comma, or in the middle of a sentence after a comma:

For example, the p.d. is 12 V when the current is 1.2 A, but 20 V when the current is 2 A.

Some metals, for instance, silver, copper and gold, are good electrical conductors.

Such as can be used after a comma, but it cannot start a sentence:

Electrical appliances, such as fridges, freezers and washing machines, have a label with a power rating.

8 Rewrite the sentences using *for example*, *for instance* or *such as*. Use the Language focus box to help you.

a Metals are good conductors of electricity. Copper and aluminium are good conductors.

....

....

b Electricity transfers energy from a source to a device. A power supply transfers energy to a lamp.

....

....

c Electrical appliances often have a label with their **power rating**. The power rating of a fridge is 1.5 kW.

....

....

d The energy transferred by an electrical appliance is measured in kWh. A 2 kW kettle used for three hours transfers 6 kWh of energy.

....

....

9 A hair dryer has a power rating of 2400 W. Janvi uses the hairdryer for 30 minutes.

a Calculate the energy transferred by the hairdryer in kWh.

....

....

b Electricity costs 15p per kWh. How much did it cost for Janvi to use her hairdryer?

....

....

> # Chapter 19
Electrical circuits

IN THIS CHAPTER YOU WILL:

Science skills:

- describe current, potential difference and resistance in series and parallel circuits

- describe electrical safety measures.

English skills:

- practise using relative clauses with relative pronouns

- practise using the modal verb *should*.

Exercise 19.1 Electrical components

IN THIS EXERCISE YOU WILL:

Science skills:

- recognise circuit symbols

- describe the functions of electrical components.

English skills:

- practise using relative clauses with relative pronouns.

KEY WORDS

generator: a device where a coil of wire rotates in a magnetic field which induces a current in the coil

transformer: a device used to change the voltage of an a.c. electricity supply

In this exercise, you will look at circuit symbols for electrical components and what the functions of the components are.

1 Match each electrical component to its circuit symbol.

Component	Symbol
A cell	1 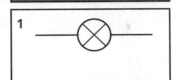
B generator	2 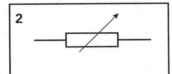
C transformer	3 
D switch	4 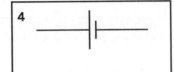
E variable resistor	5 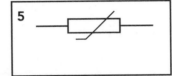
F lamp	6 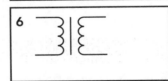
G thermistor	7 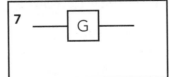

LANGUAGE FOCUS

When you describe things, places or people, you often need to give extra information. You can use the following relative pronouns to introduce different information:

who – people   that – things

where – places   when – moments in time

We learned about the scientist <u>who carried out the first experiments with electricity</u>.

This graph shows the changes <u>that we observed during our experiment</u>.

The photograph shows the point in the experiment <u>when the lamp was lit</u>.

To introduce something that belongs to a person or thing that you are describing, use whose:

We saw a film about the scientist <u>whose discoveries we were studying</u>.

2   Fill in the gaps to complete the sentences about circuit components. Use the words below. Words can be used more than once. Not all of the words are needed.

that   when   where   whose

a   A resistor is an electrical component .... is used to control the amount of current in a circuit.

b   The resistance of an NTC thermistor increases .... the temperature decreases.

c   A variable resistor is a resistor .... resistance can be changed.

d   Light-dependent resistors can be used in sensing circuits .... detect changes in light levels.

3   Write three sentences describing what an NTC thermistor is and what it can be used for. Use the relative pronouns in the Language focus box in your answer.

....

....

....

....

....

....

Exercise 19.2 Electric circuits

KEY WORDS

parallel circuit: a circuit where all the components are connected separately to the power supply

In this exercise, you will look at current, potential difference and resistance in series and **parallel circuits**.

4   Figure 19.1 shows a series circuit and a parallel circuit. Write series or parallel under the correct circuit.

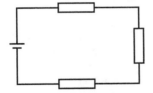 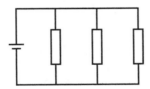

Figure 19.1: Series circuit and parallel circuit.

5   Fill in the gaps to complete the sentences about resistors in series and in parallel. Use the words below. Words can be used more than once.

current   parallel   potential difference   series

a   When two resistors of different resistances are connected in

...................., the total resistance is the sum of the two resistances.

The .... flowing through each resistor is the same. The resistor

with the largest resistance has the greatest .... across it.

b When the two resistors are connected in ...., the total resistance is less than the resistance of the smallest resistor.

The .... flowing through each resistor is less than the

.... from the power supply. The .... across each resistor is the same.

LANGUAGE FOCUS

When describing an experiment:

- start by describing how the apparatus is set up and use words giving the order in which you do things, for example, *First, Then, Before, After*

- use suitable verbs, for example, *connect, change, add, ensure*

- use the imperative if your description is in the form of instructions.

<u>*Before*</u> *switching on the power supply,* <u>*ensure*</u> *that the ammeter and voltmeter are connected correctly.*

If you want to give suggestions, use *can* + passive:

The spring <u>*can be supported*</u> *by using a clamp stand, boss and clamp.*

You will often use the passive form of other verbs in your description:

The ammeter <u>*is connected*</u> *in series.*

---

6 Figure 19.2 shows an experiment to measure current and potential difference in a series circuit with two resistors. Write instructions on how to do this experiment. Use the Language focus box to help you.

LANGUAGE TIP

You can write instructions by using an action verb to start a sentence, for example: <u>*Connect*</u> *the ammeter and voltmeter correctly.*

Variable power supply

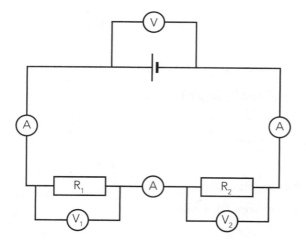

Figure 19.2: Measuring current and voltage in a series circuit.

....

....

....

....

....

....

....

....

....

....

Exercise 19.3 Electrical safety

IN THIS EXERCISE YOU WILL:

Science skills:

* describe electrical safety measures.

English skills:

* practise using the modal verb *should*.

KEY WORDS

mains electricity: the electricity supplied from power stations to homes and businesses; supplied as alternating current

fuse: a device that breaks the circuit if the current exceeds a certain value; a piece of metal wire that melts when too much current flows through it

Mains electricity can give you an electric shock if you come into contact with it. In this exercise, you will look at different electrical safety measures.

7 Find seven terms to do with electrical safety in the word string and write them on the lines below. The first one has been done for you.

neutralwireelectricalcablefusetripswitchearthwiredoubleinsulationlivewire

neutral wire ....

....

....

....

....

....

....

LANGUAGE FOCUS

To give advice, warnings or recommendations, you can use *should* with another verb. *Should* is a modal verb and needs another verb after it:

You *should always switch off* a power supply when it is not being used.

The negative form is *should not*:

You *should not touch* live electrical equipment with wet hands.

You can also use *should* with *be* + past participle, to form a passive sentence:

The power supply *should be switched* on after the circuit has been checked.

---

8 Complete these sentences about electrical safety measures, using *should* or *should not* and an appropriate verb. Use the Language focus box to help you.

a The electrical cables used in homes .... insulation around the outside so people touching the cables do not get an electric shock.

b You .... too many devices into a block adaptor as this could overload the socket and cause a fire.

c You .... a **fuse** in the plug of an electrical appliance to stop too much current flowing through the cable and damaging the cable and the circuit.

d The metal case of an electrical appliance .... to the earth wire to prevent someone getting an electric shock if there is a fault in the appliance.

9   Write a paragraph giving advice to someone on how to use a fuse.
Use the Language focus box to help you.

....

....

....

....

....

....

Electromagnetic forces

Exercise 20.1 The magnetic effect of a current

KEY WORDS

relay: a switch controlled by an electromagnet

In this exercise, you will look at the magnetic field around a current-carrying wire and how a **relay** works.

1   Fill in the gaps to complete the sentences. Use the phrases below.

   bar magnet   direction   magnetic field   right-hand grip rule

   a   When a current is passed through a wire, a .... is produced around the wire.

   b   The arrows on the magnetic field lines show the .... of the field at that particular point.

c   You can use the .... to show the direction of the magnetic field lines.

d   The pattern of magnetic field lines around a solenoid is the same as for a

....

2   Figure 20.1 shows an experiment to investigate the magnetic field around a current-carrying wire. Use the blank boxes to renumber the instructions below, so that the steps to the method are in the correct order.

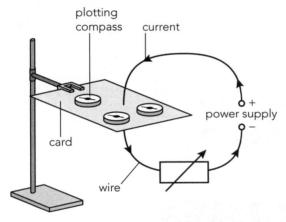

Figure 20.1: Experiment to investigate the magnetic field around a current-carrying wire.

Move the plotting compass around the wire and note the new direction of the field.   ☐

Draw the pattern of the magnetic field lines   ☐

Switch on the power supply.   ☐

Connect the wire to the power supply.   ☐

Set up the equipment as shown in the diagram.   ☐

Put a plotting compass near the wire and note the direction of the field.   ☐

3 Figure 20.2 shows a relay circuit. Explain how the magnetic effect of a current is used to turn on a motor.

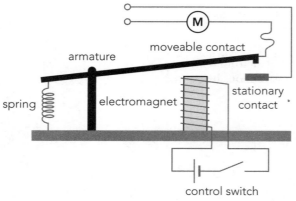

Figure 20.2: A relay circuit.

....

....

....

....

....

....

Exercise 20.2 The motor effect

IN THIS EXERCISE YOU WILL:

Science skills:

- describe the motor effect

- describe how a loudspeaker works.

English skills:

- practise using connectives of cause and effect.

KEY WORDS

motor effect: when current flows in a wire in a magnetic field which is not parallel to the current, a force is exerted on the wire

In this exercise, you will look at the **motor effect** and how a loudspeaker works.

4   Fill in the gaps to complete the sentences about the motor effect. Use the words below. Words can be used more than once.

current   force   interact   magnetic field

A .... flowing through a wire produces a ....

around the wire. If the wire is put into the .... of a permanent

magnet then the two fields .... This produces a ....
on the wire and the wire moves.

LANGUAGE FOCUS

Use connectives to link parts of sentences to make your science writing more effective. For example, *but*, *although*, *whereas*, *while*, *therefore*, and *as*. Some connectives can go at the beginning or in the middle of a sentence. *So*, *because* and *since* are also useful connectives. *Because* and *since* are similar in meaning and introduce cause. *So* introduces an effect or consequence.

Because and *since* go in front of the cause:

<u>Because</u> *a current is flowing through the wire, there is a magnetic field around the wire.*

There is a magnetic field around the wire, <u>since</u> *a current is flowing through the wire.*

So goes in front of the effect:

There is a current flowing in the wire, <u>so</u> *there is a magnetic field around the wire.*

The connective *in order to* is a useful way of introducing the reason for doing something or the aim or intention behind an action:

An iron core is used in an electromagnet in order to increase the strength of the magnetic field.

5   Figure 20.3 shows an experiment to investigate the force on a copper wire. Rewrite the sentences as one sentence using the connectives in the Language focus box.

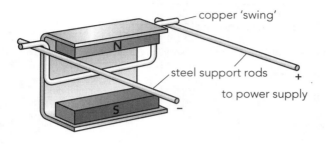

Figure 20.3: Experiment to investigate the force on a copper wire.

a   The power supply is switched on. Current flows through the steel rods and the copper wire.

   ....

b   The current flows through the copper wire. The wire has a magnetic field around it.

   ....

c   The two magnetic fields interact. The copper wire moves.

   ....

d   The direction of the current is reversed. The direction of the force on the wire is reversed.

   ....

6   Figure 20.4 shows a loudspeaker. Explain how a loudspeaker works when connected to a microphone. Use the connectives in the Language focus box in your answer.

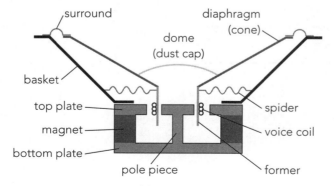

Figure 20.4: A loudspeaker.

....

....

....

....

....

....

Exercise 20.3 The electric motor

IN THIS EXERCISE YOU WILL:

Science skills:

- describe how a simple electric motor works.

English skills:

- practise using comparative adjectives.

KEY WORDS

electric motor: a device that uses the motor effect to make a coil of wire rotate

commutator: a device used to allow current to flow to and from the coil of a d.c. motor

In this exercise, you will look at how a simple **electric motor** works.

7 Find seven terms to do with electric motors in the word string and write them on the lines below. The first one has been done for you.

coilmotoreffectcommutatorturningeffectrotatecurrentbrush

coil
....

....

....

....

....

....

....

8 Figure 20.5 shows a simple electric motor. Fill in the gaps to describe how it works. Use the words below. Words can be used more than once. Not all of the words are needed.

brushes   current   force   magnetic field   motor effect

opposite   same

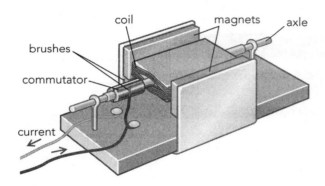

Figure 20.5: A simple electric motor.

An electric motor has a coil of wire in a .... Current flows up

the right-hand side of the coil. The .... means that this side of

the coil experiences a .... on it and it moves up. When the current

flows down the other side of the coil, it is flowing in the ....

direction. This means that the .... on this side of the coil is

in the .... direction and it moves down. The **commutator** and

.... are used to keep the current flowing in the ....
direction through the coil so it keeps rotating.

LANGUAGE FOCUS

You have seen how to form comparatives with adjectives:

A magnetic field is <u>stronger</u> near the poles of a bar magnet.

A milliammeter is <u>more sensitive than</u> an ammeter.

Sometimes, you want to say that two things change at the same time and that the changes are related. A useful structure to express these changes is:

the + comparative adjective

This structure is frequently used to give facts:

The <u>stronger</u> the magnet, the <u>larger</u> the force it exerts on a piece of iron.

Or with *will* + verb to give predictions:

The <u>larger</u> the e.m.f. of the power source, the <u>greater</u> the current <u>will be</u> in the circuit.

9   Describe the three ways of increasing the turning effect of a simple electric motor. Write complete sentences and use the structures *the* + comparative adjective and *will* + verb in your answer. Use the Language focus box to help you.

....

....

....

....

....

....

LANGUAGE TIP

Less is the opposite of *more* and *the least* is the opposite of *the most*. *More* and *most* are used more frequently than *less* or *least*.

Chapter 21

Electromagnetic induction

IN THIS CHAPTER YOU WILL:

Science skills:

- describe electromagnetic induction and how electricity is generated
- describe how electricity is transmitted and the use of transformers.

English skills:

- practise using the preposition *by*
- practise using connectives of contrast and comparative and superlative forms.

Exercise 21.1 Electromagnetic induction

IN THIS EXERCISE YOU WILL:

Science skills:

- describe electromagnetic induction.

English skills:

- practise using the preposition *by*.

KEY WORDS

induced e.m.f.: the e.m.f. created in a conductor when it cuts through magnetic field lines

In this exercise, you will look at how the motor effect works in reverse to produce an **induced e.m.f.** across an electrical conductor.

1   Complete the crossword using the clues below.

Across:

1. The work done by a cell in moving a unit charge around a circuit.

4. The region where a magnetic material feels a force.

6. A device that converts current into movement.

Down:

2. A force is exerted on current-carrying wire in a magnetic field.

3. The flow of electric charge around a circuit.

5. An electric current can flow through this material.

LANGUAGE FOCUS

By is a preposition that introduces the agent or means. The agent is the person or thing that carries out an action, while the means is the thing used to carry out an action, for example:

The <u>scientist</u> measured the current with an <u>ammeter</u>. (scientist = agent, ammeter = means)

The passive form is often used in science writing where the agent is not important:

A current was induced. (Who or what induced the current is not important.)

Sometimes, the agent is important but is not the subject of the sentence. In this case, use *by* after the passive and before the agent:

Field lines are cut <u>by the wire</u>.

It is repelled <u>by the magnet</u>.

By is also used when you want to add information about the means. In this case, use *by* + verb + *-ing*:

The scientist measured the current <u>by placing</u> an ammeter in series with the resistor.

2 Figure 21.1 shows how an e.m.f can be induced across a wire.
Rewrite each sentence using *by*. Use the Language focus box to help you.

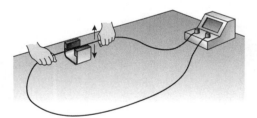

Figure 21.1: Inducing an e.m.f. using a wire.

a If you move the wire up and down in a magnetic field, this will induce an e.m.f. across the wire.

b Keeping the wire stationary and moving the magnet up and down will also produce an induced e.m.f. across the wire.

c An induced e.m.f. will cause an induced current to flow if the circuit is complete.

d When the wire is moved upwards, current will flow in one direction, and when the wire is moved downwards, it will flow in the other direction.

3 Figure 21.2 shows another way of inducing an e.m.f. across an electrical conductor. Answer the questions using complete sentences and *by* in your answers.

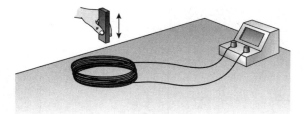

Figure 21.2: Inducing an e.m.f. using a coil of wire.

a   Explain how this set-up produces an induced e.m.f.

....

b   Describe the three ways that the strength of the induced e.m.f. can be increased.

....

....

....

Exercise 21.2 Generating and transmitting electricity

KEY WORDS

national grid: the system of power lines, pylons and transformers used to carry electricity around a country

step-up transformer: a transformer that increases the voltage of an a.c. supply

step-down transformer: a transformer that decreases the voltage of an a.c. supply

power line: cables used to carry electricity from power stations to consumers

In this exercise, you will look at generators and how electricity is transmitted from power stations to homes and businesses.

4   Fill in the gaps to complete the sentences about how a simple generator works. Use the words below. Words can be used more than once.

induced current   induced e.m.f.   magnetic field   magnets

In a generator, there are ...., which produce a ....,

and a coil of wire. When the coil of wire and the .... move relative

to each other, an .... is produced across the ends of the wire.

When the coil of wire is part of a complete circuit, an .... flows in the circuit.

LANGUAGE FOCUS

You can use connectives of contrast to express contrast between two parts of a sentence or two sentences. You have already met *while* and *whereas* and here are four more:

however   although   on the other hand   in contrast

These connectives of contrast usually begin a sentence and are followed by a comma:

In a motor, a current-carrying wire in a magnetic field experiences a force, which makes the wire rotate. However, in a generator, a wire and a magnetic field move relative to each other, which produces a current.

An induced current will flow if the wire is part of a complete circuit. In contrast, an induced current will not flow if the wire is not part of a complete circuit.

---

5   Rewrite the sentences about the **national grid** using connectives of contrast. Use the Language focus box to help you.

a   Power stations generate the electricity, which is transmitted around the country. Substations distribute the electricity to homes and businesses.

   ....

b   The electricity generated by a power station can be 25 000 V. The electricity supplied to homes is about 230 V.

   ....

c   A **step-up transformer** substation increases the voltage of the electricity. A **step-down transformer** substation decreases the voltage of the electricity.

   ....

d   In some countries, electricity is distributed to homes by **power lines** high above the ground. In other countries, electricity is distributed to homes by cables under the ground.

   ....

6 Figure 21.3 shows a national grid. Describe what happens to the voltage as the electricity is transmitted and explain why. Use connectives of contrast in your answer.

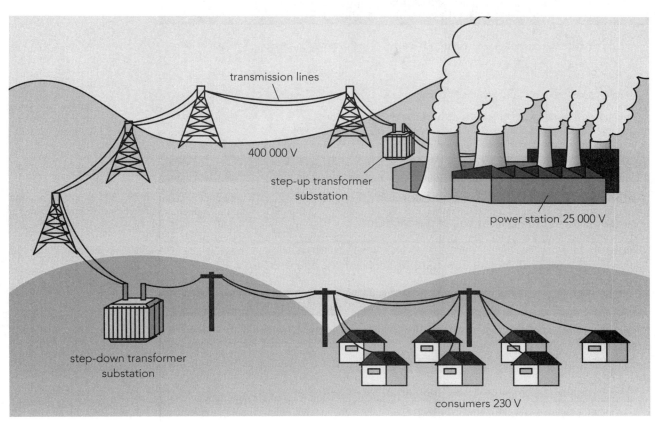

Figure 21.3: A national grid.

....

....

....

....

....

....

Exercise 21.3 Transformers

IN THIS EXERCISE YOU WILL:

Science skills:

- describe transformers.

English skills:

- practise using comparative and superlative forms.

KEY WORDS

primary coil: the input coil of a transformer

secondary coil: the output coil of a transformer

In this exercise, you will look at how transformers increase and decrease voltage.

LANGUAGE FOCUS

You have already seen how to use comparatives and superlatives to compare two or more things, for example:

more, the most   less, the least   fewer, fewest

When comparing two items, use *than* after the adjective:

Lamp A is more powerful <u>than</u> lamp B.

When comparing three or more items, use *the* before *most* or *least*:

Lamp C is <u>the most</u> powerful.

7 Fill in the gaps to complete the sentences about transformers. Use the words below:

fewer   greater   less   more   smaller

a The **primary coil** of a step-up transformer has .... turns than the **secondary coil**.

b There are .... turns on the primary coil of a step-down transformer than on the secondary coil.

c If the voltage across the primary coil of a step-down transformer is 12 V, then the voltage across the secondary coil will be ....

d When the voltage is stepped up, there is a .... current flowing in the circuit, and when the voltage is stepped down, there is a .... current flowing in the circuit.

LANGUAGE TIP

Note that, in science, *greater* and *higher* are used more frequently with numbers than *bigger*. *Lower* and *smaller* are also used.

8 Figure 21.4 shows a transformer.

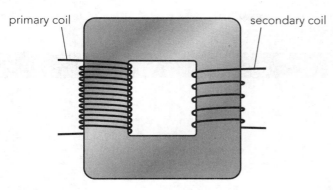

Figure 21.4: A transformer.

a State whether it is a step-up transformer or a step-down transformer.

....

b Explain how you know what type of transformer it is. Use comparatives in your answer.

....

....

9 A step-up transformer has 10 turns on the primary coil and 30 turns on the secondary coil. The voltage across the primary coil is 12 V.

a Give the transformer equation.

....

b Calculate the voltage across the secondary coil. Show your working.

Voltage across secondary coil: V

> Chapter 22
The nuclear atom

IN THIS CHAPTER YOU WILL:

Science skills:

- describe the structure of the atom, and its particles

- describe isotopes.

English skills:

- practise using adverbs of manner and time

- practise using connectives of contrast.

Exercise 22.1 The structure of the atom

IN THIS EXERCISE YOU WILL:

Science skills:

- describe the structure of the atom

- describe how the structure of the atom was discovered.

English skills:

- practise using adverbs of manner and time.

KEY WORDS

neutron: an uncharged particle found in the atomic nucleus

electron: a negatively charged particle, smaller than an atom

ionisation: when a particle (atom or molecule) becomes electrically charged by losing or gaining electrons

alpha particle: a particle made up of two protons and two neutrons; it is emitted by an atomic nucleus during radioactive decay

In this exercise, you will look at the structure of the atom and how this structure was discovered.

1　Fill in the gaps in the sentences about the structure of the atom. Use the words below. Words can be used more than once.

negatively　　nuclear model　　nucleus　　positively　　protons

In the .... of the atom, the .... of the atom is

made up of .... and **neutrons** and is .... charged.

Electrons are .... charged and orbit the ....

LANGUAGE FOCUS

You have already seen that adjectives describe things and people (nouns), and adverbs describe actions (verbs).

A powerful lightbulb shines brightly. (powerful – adjective, lightbulb – noun, shines – verb, brightly – adverb)

Adverbs of manner tell how an action happened. They go after the verb and as near to it as possible:

It shines <u>brightly</u>. It increases <u>slowly</u>. He worked <u>efficiently</u>.

To form an adverb, add *-ly* to an adjective:

bright – brightly　　slow – slowly　　efficient – efficiently

There are a few irregular adverbs, such as *hard* and *fast*.

Adverbs of time tell when an action happened:

<u>*Initially*</u>*, we thought it would break.*

The current decreased <u>eventually</u>.

Many adverbs of time also end in *-ly*, although some are expressions, such as:

in the end　　first of all　　after that

Adverbs of time go at the start or the end of the clause or sentence. If you want to use an adverb of manner (*how*) and an adverb of time (*when*) in a sentence, remember the alphabetical order (<u>m</u>anner, <u>t</u>ime):

The lightbulb shone <u>brightly after that</u>.

2　Underline the adverbs in the paragraph about forming ions. Use the Language focus box to help you.

At first, the atoms of a material have an overall neutral charge. When an atom gains an **electron**, it becomes charged negatively and forms a negative ion. When an atom loses an electron, it becomes charged positively and forms a positive ion. This process is called **ionisation**.

3   Figure 22.1 shows the experiment to investigate the structure of the atom where **alpha particles** were fired at gold foil. Answer the questions using complete sentences and adverbs.

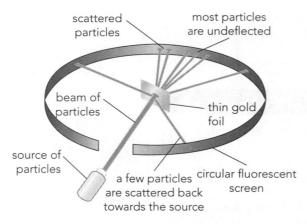

scattered particles

most particles are undeflected

beam of particles

thin gold foil

source of particles

a few particles are scattered back towards the source

circular fluorescent screen

Figure 22.1: Experiment to investigate the structure of the atom.

a   When alpha particles are fired at the gold foil, what are they expected to do?

....

....

b   Describe what happened in the experiment.

....

....

....

....

c   Give the three conclusions that were drawn from the experiment.

....

....

....

Exercise 22.2 Protons, neutrons and electrons

KEY WORDS

subatomic particle: a particle smaller than an atom

nuclide notation: the symbol for an element with its nucleon number and proton number

proton number: the number of protons in an atomic nucleus

nucleon number: the number of nucleons (protons and neutrons) in an atomic nucleus

In this exercise, you will look at the properties of **subatomic particles** and how atoms can be represented by **nuclide notation**.

4   Complete the table to show which subatomic particle is being described in each row.

Particle	Relative charge	Relative mass	Position
	0	1	in the nucleus
	−1	0	outside the nucleus
	+1	1	in the nucleus

LANGUAGE FOCUS

You have already seen that there are several expressions that you can use to express contrast:

however   *while*   *whereas*   *in contrast to*

Remember, *however* comes at the start of a sentence and a comma separates it from the rest of the sentence:

Most of the alpha particles passed straight through the gold foil.
<u>However</u>, some of the alpha particles were deflected.

While and *whereas* can go in the middle of the sentence or at the start. They have a subject and a verb after them, not a comma. *Whereas* is usually used to express two complete opposites:

<u>Whereas</u> some believed that the atom was indivisible, others believed that atoms were made up of smaller parts. (Note that 'indivisible' and 'made up of smaller parts' are opposing ideas.)

In contrast to can go anywhere in a sentence. It has a noun phrase after it, followed by a comma or a full stop, but no verb:

<u>In contrast to the plum pudding model</u>, which has electrons embedded in positive matter, the nuclear model has electrons orbiting the nucleus.

5   Rewrite the sentences about nuclide notation using expressions of contrast. Use the Language focus box to help you.

    a   The **proton number** is the number of protons in the nucleus. The **nucleon number** is the number of protons and neutrons in the nucleus.

      ....

      ....

    b   The proton number is known as the atomic number. The nucleon number is known as the mass number.

      ....

      ....

    c   An atom of carbon has six protons in its nucleus. An atom of oxygen has eight protons in its nucleus.

      ....

      ....

6   For each of the atoms below, give the number of protons, number of neutrons and number of electrons.

   a $_{11}^{23}$Na

      protons: ....

      neutrons: ....

      electrons: ....

   b $_{9}^{19}$F

      protons: ....

      neutrons: ....

      electrons: ....

   c $_{54}^{131}$Xe

      protons: ....

      neutrons: ....

      electrons: ....

Exercise 22.3 Isotopes

IN THIS EXERCISE YOU WILL:

Science skills:

*   describe isotopes.

English skills:

*   practise using key vocabulary for describing the structure of an atom.

KEY WORDS

isotope: isotopes of an element have the same proton number but different nucleon numbers

In this exercise, you will recap your knowledge about the structure of the atom and look at **isotopes**.

7 Complete the crossword.

Across:

2. A proton or neutron.

6. A particle with positive charge in the nucleus.

7. The number of protons and neutrons in the nucleus.

Down:

1. The number of protons in a nucleus.

3. A substance whose atoms all have the same number of protons.

4. The number of neutrons in a nucleus.

5. A particle with neutral charge in the nucleus.

8 Fill in the gaps to complete the sentences about isotopes. Use the words below. Words can be used more than once.

chemical   element   hydrogen   neutrons   one
protons   two

Isotopes of an element have the same numbers of .... but different numbers of .... An .... can have several isotopes. Protium, deuterium and tritium are the three isotopes of .... Protium has .... proton in its nucleus. Deuterium has .... proton and .... neutron. Tritium has .... proton and .... neutrons. These isotopes all have the same .... properties but tritium is the heaviest.

9 Two isotopes of uranium are $^{235}_{92}U$ and $^{238}_{92}U$. Write a paragraph comparing uranium-235 and uranium-238. Use the Language focus box in Exercise 22.2 to help you.

....

....

....

....

LANGUAGE TIP

Notice that certain prepositions go with particular words: *series of..., numbers of..., symbol for...*

> Chapter 23
Radioactivity

IN THIS CHAPTER YOU WILL:

Science skills:

- describe alpha, beta and gamma radiation
- describe half-life and safety issues around nuclear radiation.

English skills:

- practise using *both*, *neither*, *no*, *all*
- practise describing graphs and forming questions.

Exercise 23.1 Alpha, beta and gamma radiation

IN THIS EXERCISE YOU WILL:

Science skills:

- describe alpha, beta and gamma radiation and their properties.

English skills:

- practise using *both*, *neither*, *no*, *all*.

KEY WORDS

ionising nuclear radiation: radiation, emitted by the nucleus, which can cause ionisation; alpha or beta particles, or gamma rays

beta particle: a high-speed electron that is emitted by an atomic nucleus during radioactive decay

gamma ray: electromagnetic radiation emitted by an atomic nucleus during radioactive decay

In this exercise, you will look at the three types of **ionising nuclear radiation** and their properties.

1 Match each type of nuclear radiation with its description.

Radiation	Description
A alpha	**1** an electron; negative charge
B beta	**2** electromagnetic wave, uncharged
C gamma	**3** two protons and two neutrons; positive charge

LANGUAGE FOCUS

In science, when you talk about pairs of things, you often want to talk about their similarities:

Alpha radiation and beta radiation have a charge.

Alpha radiation and beta radiation cannot pass through concrete.

It is clearer to say:

Both alpha radiation and beta radiation have a charge.

Neither alpha radiation nor beta radiation can pass through concrete.
(Note that, because *neither* and *nor* are negative, the verb is positive.)

When you talk about more than two things, or of uncountable things (nuclear decay, for example), use *no* and *all*:

No gamma emitters change their atomic number. (Note that, because *no* is negative, the verb is positive.)

All nuclear decay is a random process.

If you want to use a pronoun (*them*, *it*, etc.) rather than a noun after *both*, *neither*, *all* or *no*, the sentences are a little different:

Both of them are charged. (*them* = alpha and beta radiation)

Neither of them can pass through concrete. (*them* = alpha and beta radiation)

None of them change their atomic number. (*them* = gamma emitters)

All of it is a random process. (*it* = nuclear decay)

2   Fill in the gaps to complete the sentences about alpha, beta and gamma radiation.
    Use the words below. Words can be used more than once.

    all   both   neither   no   nor   none

a   The three types of radiation are alpha, beta and gamma, and

    .... of them are ionising.

b   .... **beta particles** and **gamma rays** travel faster than
    alpha particles.

c   .... alpha particles .... beta particles can pass
    through a few millimetres of aluminium.

d   .... of the types of ionising nuclear radiation are completely

    safe as .... of them can cause harm to living tissue.

e   .... ionising nuclear radiation can pass through thick lead.

f   .... emissions of nuclear radiation from a nucleus are
    spontaneous and random.

3   Write a paragraph comparing the penetrating power and the ionising effect of the
    three types of nuclear radiation. Use the Language focus box to help you.

    ....

    ....

    ....

    ....

    ....

    ....

Exercise 23.2 Decay and half-life

IN THIS EXERCISE YOU WILL:

Science skills:

- describe radioactive decay and half-life.

English skills:

- practise describing and interpreting graphs.

KEY WORDS

radioactive decay: the emission of alpha, beta or gamma radiation from an unstable nucleus

half-life: the average time taken for half the nuclei in a sample of a radioactive material to decay

When a radioactive material emits alpha, beta or gamma radiation, this is known as **radioactive decay**. In this exercise, you will look at the **half-life** of a radioactive material.

4 Find seven terms to do with radioactive decay in the word string and write them on the lines below. The first one has been done for you.

   activitybetadecayradioisotopehalf-lifealphadecayrandomcountrate

activity

....

....

....

....

....

....

LANGUAGE FOCUS

In order to describe a scientific graph, you need to use specific words, for example:

Nouns: *label*, *axis* (singular), *axes* (plural), *slope*, origin

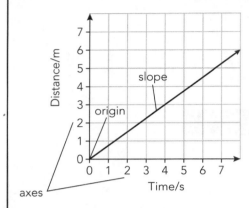

Adjectives: *straight, proportional*

Verbs: *increase, decrease, show*

Adverbs: *steadily, upwards, downwards*

Expressions: *greater than, less than, lower than, equal to, the relationship between*

For example:

The distance at 5 s is greater than the distance at 2 s.

The relationship between distance and time is directly proportional, showing that the speed is constant.

5   Figure 23.1 shows a count rate v time graph for a radioactive material.
     Fill in the gaps to complete the description of the graph. Use the words below:

axes   between   downwards   greater than   origin

proportional   shows   straight

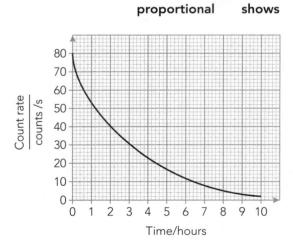

Figure 23.1: Count rate v time graph.

The graph .... the relationship .... count rate and time for a radioactive material. The .... are Count rate/counts per second and Time/hours. The line does not start at the ....
The line is not .... but curves .... This shows that count rate is not directly .... to time. The count rate at one hour is .... the count rate at five hours.

6   Figure 23.2 shows the count rate v time graph for a sample of a radioactive material.

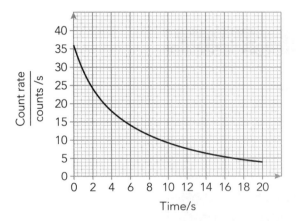

Figure 23.2: Count rate v time graph.

a   Give the half-life of the radioactive material.

    ....

b   The initial sample of the radioactive material has 920 undecayed atoms. How many atoms will be left undecayed after three half-lives? Draw a table to help you.

    Number of atoms left undecayed: ....

Exercise 23.3 Safety issues

IN THIS EXERCISE YOU WILL:

Science skills:

- describe how radioactive materials can be handled safely
- describe the effects of ionising nuclear radiation on living things.

English skills:

- practise forming questions.

KEY WORDS

radioisotope: a radioactive isotope of an element

In this exercise, you will look at the effects of ionising nuclear radiation on living tissue and how **radioisotopes** can be used and moved around safely.

7 Write 'yes' or 'no' in the table to show whether the ways of handling radioisotopes are safe or not.

Way of handling radioisotope	Handling safely?
wearing normal clothes in a contaminated area	
operating equipment from a separate room	
picking it up with your fingers	
storing it in a lead-lined box	
marking it as radioactive when it is being transported	
keeping it in an unlocked cupboard when not in use	

LANGUAGE FOCUS

It is important to recognise when a sentence is a question. Questions often have a clue at the start that tells you that it is a question. In English, there are two clues.

The question often begins with the following words (which all have w and h):

<u>wh</u>at   <u>wh</u>ich   <u>wh</u>en   <u>wh</u>ere   <u>wh</u>y   <u>wh</u>o   <u>wh</u>ose   <u>h</u>o<u>w</u>   <u>h</u>o<u>w</u> many

<u>What</u> is the radioactive material being transported in?

The auxiliary verb (do, have, be, will, can, etc.) is before the subject:

<u>Where was</u> the radioactive material transported to?

Note: Some questions with what or who do not have an auxiliary near the start, for example:

<u>What</u> happened to the radioactive material?

When you write questions and answers, it is important to use the correct form or tense of the verb. Reading a question carefully will help you choose the best tense for the answer:

<u>What is</u> the radioactive material being transported in? It is <u>being transported</u> in a lead-lined container.

<u>Where was</u> the radioactive material transported to? It <u>was transported</u> to the hospital to be used for radiation therapy.

<u>What happened</u> to the radioactive material? It <u>was disposed</u> of safely after it was used.

8   Fill in the gaps to complete the questions and answers. Use the words below:

divide   ionisation   kill   offspring   tumour
what   which   why

a   *Question:* .... is an intense dose of radiation dangerous?

Answer: It can cause a lot of .... in a cell, which can

.... the cell.

b   *Question:* .... could happen if the DNA in a cell nucleus was damaged?

Answer: The cell could start to .... uncontrollably, which could cause a ....

   c   *Question:* If an egg cell or sperm cell is damaged, the damaged DNA can be

passed on to the animal's ....

Answer: If an egg cell or sperm cell is damaged, the damaged DNA can be

passed on to the animal's ....

9   Answer the following questions with complete sentences, using the correct forms of the verbs in the question. Use the Language focus box to help you.

   a   Which of the following types of nuclear radiation is the most ionising – alpha, beta or gamma?

....

....

   b   Why are humans least likely to be harmed by alpha radiation coming from outside the body?

....

....

   c   What can happen if you breathe in radon gas, which emits alpha radiation?

....

....

Chapter 24

Earth and the Solar System

IN THIS CHAPTER YOU WILL:

Science skills:

- describe the Earth and the Moon
- describe the Solar System and the objects in it.

English skills:

- practise using pronouns
- practise using the *-ing* form of verbs.

Exercise 24.1 The Earth and the Moon

IN THIS EXERCISE YOU WILL:

Science skills:

- describe day and night, and the seasons
- describe the phases of the Moon.

English skills:

- practise using pronouns.

KEY WORDS

phases of the Moon: the different ways the Moon looks when viewed from Earth over a period of one month

axis: the imaginary line between the Earth's North and South poles

orbit: the path of an object as it moves around a larger object

Equator: the imaginary line drawn round the Earth halfway between the North Pole and the South Pole

In this exercise, you will look at how the motion of the Earth causes day and night, and the seasons, and how the motion of the Moon causes the **phases of the Moon**.

LANGUAGE FOCUS

You often find the pronouns *they*, *it*, *them*, *their* and *its* in scientific texts. These pronouns are used so that nouns do not have to be repeated. When you see *it*, *its*, *they*, *their* or *them* in a text, find and circle the nouns they refer to.

Pluto was discovered in 1930. Scientists classified [1]it as a planet until 2006, when [2]they reclassified [3]it as a dwarf planet. [4]Its moons include Charon, Nix and Hydra. The best known of [5]them is Charon.

([1]*it* = Pluto   [2]*they* = scientists   [3]*it* = Pluto   [4]*Its* = Pluto's   [5]*them* = moons)

In the text above, there are five pronouns. All the singular pronouns (*it* and *its*) mean Pluto. The two plural pronouns (*they* and *them*) refer to different things – scientists and moons. How do you know what they refer to? Look in front of the pronoun for the nearest subject or object in the plural. If the subject or object makes logical sense, then it is the noun being referred to. For example, look in front of [2]*they*, and you find *scientists*. Look in front of [5]*them*, and you find *Charon, Nix* and *Hydra*. Remember not to use a pronoun the first time you mention something.

1 Fill in the gaps in the sentences. Use the words below. Words can be used more than once. Not all the words need to be used.

it   its   their   them   they

a The Sun appears to rise in the east and .... appears to set in the west.

b Day and night are caused by the Earth spinning on .... **axis** and .... rotates once every 24 hours.

c When countries are on the side of the Earth facing the Sun, ... people experience day, but when .... are on the side facing away from the Sun, the people experience night.

2 Rewrite the sentences, replacing the underlined nouns with pronouns.

a The Earth **orbits** the Sun and the Earth takes just over 365 days for one orbit.

....

b There are seasons on the Earth because the Earth is tilted on the Earth's axis..

....

c Countries at the **Equator** do not have seasons because the rays from the Sun always incident on the countries at the same angle.

....

LANGUAGE TIP

Note that you can use *they/them/their* + plural verb to refer to one person when gender is not important in the context, or if they ask you to use *they/them/their*. Using *they* is frequent in science.

d <u>The Moon</u> orbits the Earth every 27.5 days and the part of <u>the Moon</u> that faces the Sun is illuminated.

....

e The Moon has phases because the shape of the illuminated part of <u>the Moon</u> changes as <u>the Moon</u> orbits.

....

3 Read the text then complete the table with the nouns that pronouns 1–6 are referring to.

> The planet Jupiter has a shorter day than the Earth. [1]Its rotation on [2]its axis takes about ten hours. However, [3]it has a much longer year of about 4380 days. The planets beyond the Earth in the Solar System have longer years because [4]they are further from the Sun than the Earth. It takes [5]them longer to orbit the Sun. Planets closer to the Sun have shorter years as it takes [6]them less time to orbit the Sun.

Pronoun	What is it referring to
1	
2	
3	
4	
5	
6	

Exercise 24.2 The Solar System

IN THIS EXERCISE YOU WILL:

Science skills:

- describe the Solar System and the objects in it.

English skills:

- practise using key vocabulary to do with the Solar System.

> **KEY WORDS**
>
> **meteoroid:** a lump of rock that orbits the Sun

In this exercise, you will look at the Solar System, and the planets and other objects in the Solar System.

4   Link each key term with its definition.

Term		Definition
A asteroid		**1** a frozen ball of dust, gas and rock that orbits the Sun
B planet		**2** a small, round, rocky object that orbits a planet
C comet		**3** a lump of rock that orbits the Sun
D moon		**4** a large round object that orbits the Sun

5   Figure 24.1 shows an artist's impression of the Solar System. Fill in the gaps to complete the sentences. Use the words below.

asteroids   eight   gas   inner   minor   moons   outer
rocky   Sun   Uranus   Venus

Figure 24.1: The Solar System.

The Solar System consists of the .... and the ....
planets that orbit it. Mercury, ..., Earth and Mars are the
.... planets and are .... and small. Jupiter, Saturn,
.... and Neptune are the .... planets and are huge
balls of .... Pluto used to be a planet but has been reclassified
as a .... planet. Most of the planets have ....
orbiting them. There are other smaller objects that orbit the Sun, including
..........................., **meteoroids** and comets.

6   Describe how scientists think the planets were formed. Use pronouns in your
    answer. Use the Language focus box in Exercise 24.1 to help you.

....

....

....

....

....

....

Exercise 24.3 Forces in the Solar System

IN THIS EXERCISE YOU WILL:

Science skills:

* describe forces in the Solar System

* calculate the time it takes for light to reach distant objects.

English skills:

* practise using the *-ing* form of verbs.

KEY WORDS

inner planet: the four planets nearest the Sun in the Solar System, which are Mercury, Venus, Earth and Mars

outer planet: the four planets furthest from the Sun in the Solar System, which are Jupiter, Saturn, Uranus and Neptune

In this exercise, you will look at forces in the Solar System and the time it takes for light to reach distant objects.

LANGUAGE FOCUS

You have already looked at the *-ing* form of a verb. It can be used in different ways.

As a noun:

Stargazing is becoming more and more popular.

Do you like stargazing?

After a preposition:

He is very interested in learning more about the Solar System.

Scientists are looking into building solar farms in space.

After some verbs, e.g. *avoid, begin, start, stop, try*:

We want to try calculating the diameter of the Sun.

We should stop recording data for the experiment.

After when (meaning *when you are / it is / they are*):

When calculating the distance of a planet from the Earth, you need to remember that they are both in orbit.

After a noun, or a word such as *something, everything* or *anything* (meaning *who is / which is / who are / which are*):

Some scientists studying our galaxy are researching gravitational lensing.

Anything re-entering the Earth's atmosphere needs to be able to cope with very high temperatures.

7   Complete the table with the *-ing* form of the verb.

Verb	*-ing* form
to orbit	
to find	
to point	
to travel	
to have	
to pull	

8   Fill in the gaps to complete the sentences using the *-ing* forms of the verbs below.

decrease   **have**   **increase**   **orbit**

a   The Sun .... the most mass of any object in the Solar System means that its gravitational field strength is larger than that of any other object in the Solar System.

b   Objects .... around the Sun are kept in their orbits by the Sun's gravitational force.

c   .... the mass of an object increases its gravitational field strength, so more massive planets have stronger gravitational fields at their surface.

d   Because of gravitational field strength .... with distance, the **inner planets** experience a greater gravitational force from the Sun than the **outer planets**.

9 The table shows the average distance of three planets from the Sun. Complete the
table to show the time it takes for light from the Sun to reach each planet.
Note the speed of light in a vacuum is 300 000 000 m/s.

Planet	Average distance from the Sun/m	Time for light to reach the planet from the Sun/s
Mercury	58 000 000 000	
Saturn	1427 000 000 000	
Neptune	4497 000 000 000	

Show your working in the space below.

> Chapter 25
Stars and the Universe

IN THIS CHAPTER YOU WILL:

Science skills:

- describe stars and galaxies
- describe redshift and the Big Bang theory.

English skills:

- practise using adjectives and adverbs, and definite and indefinite articles
- practise using plural noun forms.

Exercise 25.1 The Sun

IN THIS EXERCISE YOU WILL:

Science skills:

- describe the Sun.

English skills:

- practise using adjectives and adverbs.

KEY WORDS

plasma: a completely ionised gas in which the temperature is too high for neutral atoms to exist so it consists of electrons and positively-charged atomic nuclei

In this exercise, you will look at the Sun, what it is made of and what it radiates.

LANGUAGE FOCUS

Adjectives only have one form in English. They go in front of the noun they are describing:

a dwarf planet   a new star   a distant galaxy

Or, they go after the verbs *be*, *become* or *turn*.

*It is fascinating.   It becomes colder at night.
The sky turns red at sunset.*

Most adverbs come after the verbs they are describing:

It orbits slowly around its star.   It heats up gradually.

Some adverbs can go at the start or end of a sentence.

*Suddenly, it explodes.   The star seems to disappear quickly.
Eventually, it cools.*

1 Write each word in the correct column in the table to show whether it is an adjective or an adverb.

medium   gradually   dense   quickly   violently   cool

highly   glowing   large   nearly   gaseous   generally

Adjective	Adverb

2 a Fill in the gaps in the paragraph about the Sun. Use the words below. Words can be used more than once.

gas   helium   hot   hydrogen   medium   solar mass

stable   visible light   ultraviolet

The Sun is a .... star, and is a huge glowing ball of

.... The Sun is extremely .... and nearly all

of it is **plasma**. The Sun is mostly made up of .... but it also

has 24% .... and a small amount of other heavier elements.

The Sun is a .... mass star and the mass of the Sun is known

as a .... The Sun continually radiates ....,

infrared radiation and .... radiation.

b (Circle) the adjectives and underline the adverbs in the paragraph in part **a**.

3 Describe how stars like the Sun are powered. Use adjectives and adverbs in
your answer.

....

....

....

....

....

....

Exercise 25.2 Galaxies

IN THIS EXERCISE YOU WILL:

Science skills:

- describe galaxies
- describe how astronomers measure distances in space.

English skills:

- practise using definite and indefinite articles.

KEY WORDS

light-year: the distance travelled in space by light in one year

In this exercise, you will look at galaxies and how astronomers measure distances in space.

4 Find eight terms in the word string and write them on the lines below. The first one has been done for you.

starMilkyWaygravityparallaxspiralgalaxydistanceProximaCentaurilight-year

star
....

....

....

....

LANGUAGE FOCUS

The word *the* is called the definite article. There is only one form:

the planet   *the* planets   *the* Milky Way

It has several different uses:

When there is only one of something, or everyone knows which one you are talking about:

Look at *the* Milky Way. (There is only one Milky Way.)

Look at *the* Moon. (There are many moons in the Solar System, but the Earth only has one.)

When you use a superlative adjective or before the adjective *only*:

Mercury is *the nearest* planet to the Sun.

Earth is *the only* planet in the habitable zone.

When something has been mentioned before using the indefinite articles *a* or *an*:

We carried out *an* experiment. The aim of *the* experiment was to find the diameter of Venus.

At the start of a phrase with *of* or *in* + noun:

The study *of* physics related to stars and the Universe is called astrophysics.

The largest planet *in* the Solar System is Jupiter.

5   Complete the sentences with the correct definite or indefinite articles.
    Use the Language focus box to help you.

a   .... galaxy is .... group of stars that have been
pulled together by .... force of gravity and there are billions
of galaxies in .... Universe.

b   Our Solar System, which includes .... Sun, is found in
.... spiral arm of .... Milky Way galaxy.

c   .... Milky Way galaxy is .... flat disc
with .... bulge at .... centre and has
.... diameter of about 100 000 **light-years**.

d   .... light from .... Sun takes eight minutes to
get to .... Earth, while .... light from Proxima
Centauri, our next nearest star, takes .... much longer time of
4.2 light-years.

> **LANGUAGE TIP**
>
> Note: *the* refers to something specific, so it is not appropriate if you want to make a generalisation: *Meteorites hitting the Earth are thought to have caused some of the biggest changes to life on Earth.*

Exercise 25.3 Redshift and the Big Bang theory

IN THIS EXERCISE YOU WILL:

Science skills:

- describe redshift and the Big Bang theory.

English skills:

- practise using plural forms of nouns.

KEY WORDS

redshift: an increase in the observed wavelength of electromagnetic radiation (including visible light) from a star or galaxy because it is moving away from us

Big Bang theory: the Universe (space, time, matter, energy) was created at a single point 13.8 billion years ago and has been expanding and cooling ever since

The Universe is made up of billions of galaxies. In this exercise, you will look at **redshift** and how it is evidence for the **Big Bang theory**.

LANGUAGE FOCUS

Most plural nouns in English are formed by adding -s or -es to the singular noun:

wave – waves   physicist – physicists

If a singular noun ends with a consonant and a -y, the -y becomes -ie before you add the -s:

frequency – frequencies   activity – activities

Some scientific words are from Latin or Greek and have different endings.

Nouns ending in -us in the singular form usually end with -i in the plural form:

nucleus – nuclei   radius – radii

Nouns ending -a in the singular form may end with -ae in the plural form:

antenna – antennae   formula – formulae

Nouns ending in -is in the singular form usually end with -es in the plural form:

axis – axes   analysis – analyses

Nouns ending in -on or -um in the singular form may end with -a in the plural form:

criterion – criteria   phenomenon – phenomena

6   Complete the table to show the plural of each noun.

Noun	Plural
theory	
stimulus	
crisis	
curriculum	
ellipsis	
half	

7   Explain how redshift is evidence for the Big Bang theory. Use the correct plurals in your answer.

....

....

....

....

....

....

> Glossary

Command Words

Below are the Cambridge International definitions for command words that may be used in exams. The information in this section is taken from the Cambridge IGCSE™ Physics syllabus (0625/0972) for examination from 2023. You should always refer to the appropriate syllabus document for the year of your examination to confirm the details and for more information. The syllabus document is available on the Cambridge International website. www.cambridgeinternational.org

calculate: work out from given facts, figures or information

comment: give an informed opinion

compare: identify / comment on similarities and / or differences

deduce: conclude from available information

define: give precise meaning

describe: state the points of a topic / give characteristics and main features

determine: establish an answer using the information available

explain: set out purposes or reasons / make the relationships between things evident / provide why and / or how and support with relevant evidence

give: produce an answer from a given source or recall / memory

identify: name / select / recognise

justify: support a case with evidence / argument

predict: suggest what may happen based on available information

sketch: make a simple freehand drawing showing the key features, taking care over proportions

state: express in clear terms

suggest: apply knowledge and understanding to situations where there are a range of valid responses in order to make proposals/put forward considerations

Key Words

acceleration: the rate of change of an object's speed

acceleration of free fall: the acceleration of an object falling freely under gravity

alpha particle: a particle made up of two protons and two neutrons; it is emitted by an atomic nucleus during radioactive decay

amplitude: the greatest height or depth of a wave from its undisturbed position

anticlockwise: turning in the opposite direction from the hands on a clock

atmospheric pressure: the pressure felt by an object in the Earth's atmosphere due to particles in the air colliding with it

average speed: the speed calculated from total distance travelled divided by total time taken

axis: the imaginary line between the Earth's North and South poles

bar magnet: a rectangular permanent magnet with a north pole at one end and a south pole at the other end

base: lowest part of a structure in contact with a surface

beta particle: a high-speed electron that is emitted by an atomic nucleus during radioactive decay

Big Bang theory: the Universe (space, time, matter, energy) was created at a single point 13.8 billion years ago and has been expanding and cooling ever since

bimetallic strip: two different metals joined together

biomass fuel: a renewable energy resource made from plant matter or animal waste; also known as a biofuel

Brownian motion: the motion of small particles suspended in a liquid or gas, caused by molecular bombardment

cathode ray oscilloscope: an instrument that shows a sound wave as a trace (line) on a screen

cell: a device that provides an electromotive force in a circuit

centre of gravity: all the mass of an object is considered to be located here

changes of state: changing from one state of matter to another

clockwise: turning in the same direction as the hands on a clock

commutator: a device used to allow current to flow to and from the coil of a d.c. motor

contact force: the force between two objects that are touching

convection: the transfer of thermal energy through a material by the movement of the material itself

convection current: the transfer of thermal energy by the motion of a fluid

critical angle: the minimum angle of incidence at which total internal reflection occurs

deceleration: slowing down; a negative acceleration

deform: changing the size or shape of an object

density: the ratio of mass per unit volume for a substance

diffraction: when a wave spreads out as it travels through a gap or past the edge of an object

distance–time graph: a graph showing the motion of an object with time on the x-axis and distance on the y-axis

e.m.f.: the electrical work done by a source (cell, battery, etc.) in moving (a unit) charge around a circuit

efficiency: the fraction (or percentage) of energy supplied that is usefully transferred

electric motor: a device that uses the motor effect to make a coil of wire rotate

electrical conductor: a material that allows the flow of electrons (electric current)

electrical insulator: a material that does not allow the flow of electrons (electric current)

electromagnet: a coil of wire that acts as a magnet when an electric current passes through it

electromagnetic spectrum: the spectrum of all the wavelengths of electromagnetic waves

electron: a negatively charged particle, smaller than an atom

electrostatic charge: a property of an object that causes it to attract or repel other objects with charge

energy: quantity that must be changed or transferred to make something happen

evaporation: changing from a liquid to a gas at any temperature

event: something that happens or takes place, often at a specific time and place

Equator: the imaginary line drawn round the Earth halfway between the North Pole and the South Pole

equilibrium: when no net force and no net moment act on an object

extension: the increased length of an object when a load is attached to it

fiducial marker: a mark used to identify the number of rotations

fluid: a liquid or a gas

force: the action of one body on a second body

fossil fuels: natural gas, coal and oil; a non-renewable source of energy

frequency: the number of complete vibrations or waves per unit time

fuse: a device that breaks the circuit if the current exceeds a certain value; a piece of metal wire that melts when too much current flows through it

gamma ray: electromagnetic radiation emitted by an atomic nucleus during radioactive decay

generator: a device where a coil of wire rotates in a magnetic field which induces a current in the coil

gradient: the slope of a line on a graph

gravitational field strength: the gravitational force exerted per unit mass placed at that point

gravitational potential energy: the energy that an object has when it is raised up against the gravitational force

half-life: the average time taken for half the atoms in a sample of a radioactive material to decay

hazard: something that could potentially cause someone harm or cause them to become ill

hydroelectric power: using the kinetic energy of water to turn a turbine attached to a generator, which generates electricity

immerse: to cover something in a fluid (usually water) so that the object is submerged

induced e.m.f.: the e.m.f. created in a conductor when it cuts through magnetic field lines

infrared radiation: electromagnetic radiation with a wavelength greater than that of visible light; sometimes known as thermal energy radiation

inner planet: the four planets nearest the Sun in the Solar System, which are Mercury, Venus, Earth and Mars

instantaneous speed: the speed at a particular moment in time

ionisation: when a particle (atom or molecule) becomes electrically charged by losing or gaining electrons

ionising nuclear radiation: radiation, emitted by the nucleus, which can cause ionisation; alpha or beta particles, or gamma rays

isotope: isotopes of an element have the same proton number but different nucleon numbers

kinetic particle model of matter: a model in which matter consists of moving particles

laterally inverted: reversed left to right

light-year: the distance travelled in space by light in one year

lines of force: a way to represent force in an electric field

load: the force stretching an object

longitudinal wave: a wave in which the particles vibrate backwards and forwards, along the direction of travel of the wave

magnetic field: the region of space around a magnet or electric current in which a magnetic pole experiences a force

magnetic field lines: lines that represent the direction the magnetic force would have on the north pole of a magnet

mains electricity: the electricity supplied from power stations to homes and businesses; supplied as alternating current

mass: the quantity of matter in an object

meteoroid: a lump of rock that orbits the Sun

moment: the turning effect of a force about a pivot

motor effect: when current flows in a wire in a magnetic field which is not parallel to the current, a force is exerted on the wire

national grid: the system of power lines, pylons and transformers used to carry electricity around a country

neutron: an uncharged particle found in the atomic nucleus

north pole: the magnetic pole of a magnet that points towards the Earth's North Pole

nuclear fuel: a material, such as uranium or plutonium, that undergoes radioactive decay

nucleon number: the number of nucleons (protons and neutrons) in an atomic nucleus

nuclide notation: the symbol for an element with its nucleon number and proton number

orbit: the path of an object as it moves around a larger object

outer planet: the four planets furthest from the Sun in the Solar System, which are Jupiter, Saturn, Uranus and Neptune

parallel circuit: a circuit where all the components are connected separately to the power supply

period: the time taken for one complete wave to pass a particular point

phases of the Moon: the different ways the Moon looks when viewed from Earth over a period of one month

pivot: the fixed point about which a lever turns

plasma: a completely ionised gas in which the temperature is too high for neutral atoms to exist so it consists of electrons and positively-charged atomic nuclei

plotting compass: a small compass with a needle that lines up with magnetic field lines

potential difference: the work done by (a unit) charge passing through an electrical component

power: the rate at which energy is transferred or work is done

power line: cables used to carry electricity from power stations to consumers

power rating: the maximum amount of energy that an appliance transfers per second when the appliance is being used

power station: an industrial facility where electricity is generated from fossil

pressure: the force acting per unit area at right angles to a surface

primary coil: the input coil of a transformer

principal focus: the point at which rays of light parallel to the principal axis converge after passing through a converging lens

principle of conservation of energy: energy cannot be created or destroyed; it can only be stored or transferred

principle of moments: when an object is in equilibrium, the sum of anticlockwise moments about any point equals the sum of clockwise moments about the same point

process: a series of actions or steps, often taking place over a long period of time

proton number: the number of protons in an atomic nucleus

radioactive decay: the emission of alpha, beta or gamma radiation from an unstable nucleus

radioisotope: a radioactive isotope of an element

range of frequency: the difference between the highest and the lowest frequency

rarefaction: a region where the particles of the wave are closer together

ray diagram: a diagram showing the path of a ray of light

redshift: an increase in the observed wavelength of electromagnetic radiation (including visible light) from a star or galaxy because it is moving away from us

reflection: the change of direction of a ray when it strikes the surface of a material without passing through it

refraction: the bending of light when it passes from one medium to another

relay: a switch controlled by an electromagnet

renewable energy resource: an energy resource that can be replaced when it is used, such as solar power, water waves and biofuels

resistance: a measure of how difficult it is for an electric current to flow through a device or a component in a circuit

resultant force: the single force that has the same effect on a body as two or more forces

ripple tank: a shallow water tank used to demonstrate how waves behave

secondary coil: the output coil of a transformer

series circuit: a circuit where all the components are connected in a line with each other and the power source

short range communication: wireless communication over a very short distance

SI unit: the Système International d'Unités is the internationally agreed system of units for scientists all over the world

south pole: the magnetic pole of a magnet that points towards the Earth's South Pole

speed: the distance travelled by an object per unit of time

speed–time graph: a graph showing the motion of an object with time on the x-axis and speed on the y-axis

stable: an object that is unlikely to fall over, often because it has a low centre of gravity and a wide base

states of matter: solid, liquid or gas

step-down transformer: a transformer that decreases the voltage of an a.c. supply

step-up transformer: a transformer that increases the voltage of an a.c. supply

subatomic particle: a particle smaller than an atom

tensile force: the stretching force acting on an object

thermal conductor: a substance that conducts thermal energy

thermal expansion: the increase in volume of a material when its temperature rises

thermal insulator: a substance that conducts very little thermal energy

transformer: a device used to change the voltage of an a.c. electricity supply

transmit (sound): sound energy is transferred from one place to another

unstable: an object that is likely to fall over, often because it has a high centre of gravity and a narrow base

vacuum: a space with no particles in it

variable: a quantity that can be different values

volume: the space occupied by an object

watt: the unit of power; one watt is equal to one joule of energy transferred per second

weight: the force of gravity that acts on the object

work done: the amount of energy transferred when a force moves an object through a distance in the direction of the force

> Acknowledgements

The authors and publishers acknowledge the following sources of copyright material and are grateful for the permissions granted. Thanks to the following for permission to reproduce images:

Cover scanrail/Getty Images; *Inside* mikroman6/Getty Images; tiburonstudios/Getty Images; Mykola Sosiukin/Getty Images; RusN/ Getty Images; Giphotostock/Science Photo Libarary; Science Photo Library; Wavebreakmedia/Getty Images; Universal History Archive/ Getty Images; rwarnick/Getty Images